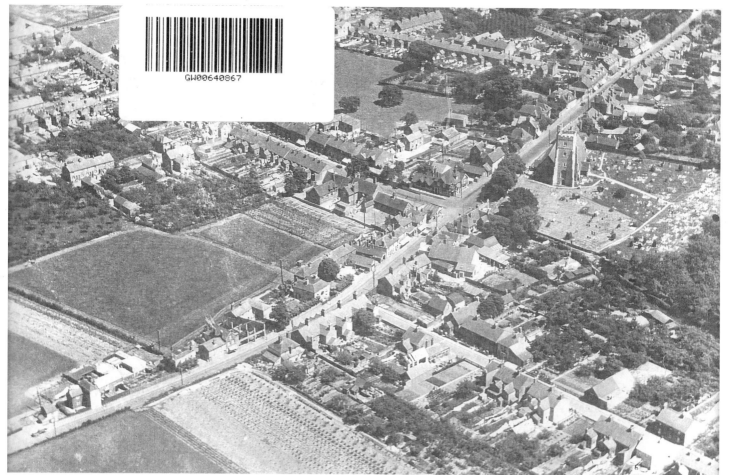

Until after the railway came to Rainham in 1858 there was little growth or development and the village remained a collection of a few outlying farms and larger houses surrounding the cottages of the High Street, Pudding Road and the school at the very top of Whitehorse Lane (Station Road) clustered around the church. By 1897, however, several new roads had been constructed and many houses built. These included Station Road, Ivy Street and the beginnings of Orchard Street. This aerial photograph shows Rainham still much the same size as in 1897 when it was taken in 1928 just before Gillingham began to fulfil the programme of promised improvements, one of which was to install main drainage. Until this and electricity were provided Rainham could not grow. Once these were in place rapid development was possible. It was stemmed briefly by the Second World War but then really took off from the 1950s. See the population graph on page 2.

THE PLACE TO SPEND A PLEASANT AFTERNOON.

RAINHAM.

C. SHAW (PROPRIETOR).

The Cricketers Inn & Tourist Hotel is seen here before the 1930s when the present building was constructed behind this building which was then demolished. The Tickham Hunt occasionally met at the Cricketers. On one such day probably in 1913 the huntsmen in their pink coats made a fine sight. Mrs Helena Thomas who would have been four years old remembers following them on foot up the landway beside the Inn to the woods in Maidstone Road. They continued down a woodland path to the green hill which was called the den and up the other side of Mierscourt valley to Chapel Lane (now called Mierscourt Road). A path then led south through the woods past the Reeve's Cottage (in the section of Mierscourt Road cut off when the bend was straightened) to a track that led to Farthing Corner. Here she and her Grandfather gave up as this was a long enough walk for both of them and they still had to walk back to Rainham. Notice the policeman in the centre of the picture. You never had to look far for the long arm of the law. There was always a policeman in this spot ready to sort out any problems and quite prepared to discipline unruly youths with a clip round the ear if necessary.

Rainham in 1921

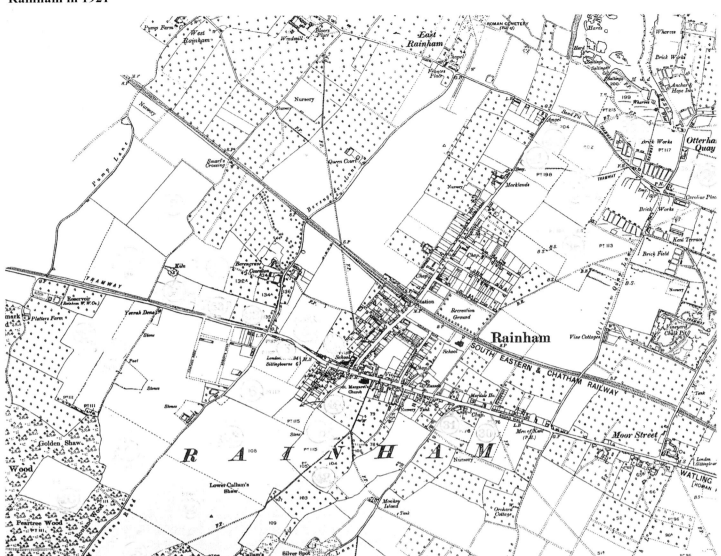

A diagrammatic representation of the population growth of Rainham from 1801 - 2001
(1801 - 722 people, 2001 - 48,712 people)

Year	
1801	_
1811	_
1821	—
1831	—
1841	—
1851	—
1861	—
1871	—
1881	—
1891	—
1901	—
1911	—
1921	—
1931	—
1941	—
1951	—
1961	—
1971	—
1981	—
1991	—
2001	—

The milestone that used to stand near Lloyds Bank, current whereabouts unknown.

Rainham High Street looking east from the Church c1906

For hundreds of years before the coming of the railway Rainham was a village straggling for about half a mile along the ancient road from Dover to London. A series of outpost settlements circled the village and were connected by footpaths, like the spokes of a wheel, to the church at its centre. It is still possible to trace some of this network of footpaths on a modern Ordnance Survey map although many paths have been absorbed into the new road layout as modern housing estates were constructed. The footpaths to Meresborough, Otterham Quay and Lower Rainham are still visible however. These three pictures give some indication of life in Rainham some hundred or so years ago. The busiest part of the village was from Station Road eastwards to Mierscourt Road. Here there were shops, the school, public houses, Doctors' surgeries, the Vicarage and Post Office and all the necessities for life. It was in this area that the first new roads were constructed, Ivy Street and Pudding Road.

Rainham High Street looking east from Pudding Road c1906

For many years Rainham had The Old Parsonage (now a fitness centre) and The Vicarage side by side. The Vicarage is just visible on the left-hand side of the top picture, opposite the Green Lion. The reason for this duplication stems from the time of Henry VIII. Before 1536 when Henry suppressed the monasteries the parsonage belonged to the Abbot of Leeds, who originally built it for the parson appointed by the Abbot to look after the spiritual needs of the people of Rainham. All the property belonging to Leeds Abbey including the eighteen acres on which both Rainham church and the parsonage were built, having been given to the monks by Robert de Crevecoeur in 1137, was confiscated in 1536. This now belonged to the King. When Elizabeth came to the throne she let the parsonage for £16 a year to the Moyle family and later sold it with the tithe lands to this family. Without a home for their Vicar, the parishioners raised the necessary money to build a vicarage and put it right next door to the parsonage.

Rainham High Street looking west from Durland House c1906

In the 1908 Kelly's Directory Rainham is described as a populous parish and village situated on the main road from Sittingbourne to Chatham, and possessing a station on the South-East & Chatham Railway. At that time the parish was in the North-Kent Parliamentary Division, the Hundred and Union of Milton and the Sittingbourne Petty Sessional Division and County Court. The acreage of the parish was: Land 3,562 acres; water one acre; tidal water 51 acres; and foreshore 414 acres. There were two and a half miles of main road in the parish and fourteen and a half miles of district roads. The population in 1901 at the last census had been 3,693 but by 1908 was estimated at over 4,000. The soil was reported as loam with chalk as the subsoil. Bricks and cement were manufactured in the district but agriculture was the largest employer. The principal crops were fruit (mainly cherries), hops and wheat, but there were at that time a number of large market gardens. The southern part of the parish was mostly woodland. The principal landowners were Lord Hothfield, who was lord of the manor, Mr E.J. Wingham Stratford, and the Governors of St Katherine's Hospital. Sir Henry Nevill Dering, Bart. was the lay impropriator of the tithes. The parish had been inhabited since ancient times and was formerly known as 'Renham'.

4073 Rainham Mark, London Road.

Rainham Mark

Rainham Mark is the boundary on Watling Street between Rainham and Gillingham. A small community grew up at this spot where two of the oldest cottages were built of chalk blocks. Mark is derived from the old English word 'mearc' meaning a boundary. When the trams arrived in 1906 the tracks were conveniently sited away from other traffic along the broad verge which still bounds the road between Gillingham and Rainham. It is now usually a bright show of crocus and daffodils in the spring. However because several buildings hugged the road at Rainham Mark the trams had to swing out from the security of their separate track into the centre of the road to negotiate this stretch of their journey.

This, combined with the slope of White Hill, often provided an eventful journey from Chatham.

In February 1925 the East Kent Gazette reported an accident at Rainham Mark. A load of bread being motored from Rainham to C&F Glass's Gillingham branch was in collision with a milk cart which suddenly cut across the front of the car to turn into a side road. Both shafts of the cart were broken, much milk was spilt, the driver was thrown out and the whole of the cart went over him. He was treated by Dr Irby Webster.

By the time of this picture in the 1950s the trams have disappeared. They ceased to run on September 30th 1930 and were replaced by the Chatham Traction Buses (the brown buses). The road has been widened and footpaths added. In the 1930s the garage and coachworks were kept by Reg Hodges, who later played a prominent part in the ARP during World War II. At this time Rainham Mark supported Bunyards General Shop, which sold oil and hardware and was entered via garage type doors, a butcher, greengrocer, newsagent and furniture store. Some of the buildings are still recognisable but the garage has gone. It was replaced by a petrol station, which in turn closed in 2005.

Rainham Mark Social Club still occupies the same building. This is the house on the left of the top photograph and it could have been a club even then, as there appears to be a notice board and advertising to the right of the gate.

The Belisha Beacon Public House at Rainham Mark sadly no longer sports its distinctive sign having been renamed 'The Hop and Vine' in a refit several years ago.

THE BELISHA BEACON, RAINHAM, KENT.

The £395 Easi-Run Villas of Hawthorne Avenue

The Easi-Run Villas in Hawthorne Avenue were built in the 1930s and advertised widely to attract new home owners. On the other side of the main road the well known local personalities of Mr Harvey and Mr Jelly had plans prepared for the Rainham Mark Building Estate comprising Edwin, Marshall and Sylvan Roads. It will probably be no surprise to learn their full names, Marshall Harvey and Edwin Jelly. They were successful in selling plots to private investors wishing to build homes for themselves. This contrasts with several proposed estates in our area which had elaborate plans drawn but failed to find purchasers.

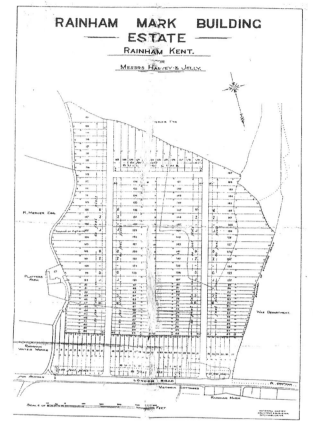

Hawthorn Avenue, Reinham Mark.

White Hill Pumping Station

Originally the water supply for Rainham was piped from Keycol. This was turned off at night with disastrous consequences in May 1892 when fire broke out during the early hours at the White Horse Public House. The Chatham Brigade, who attended, could not obtain any water and consequently the building was completely destroyed.

Later two reservoirs were built to supply the village, one at the top of White Hill opposite Pump Lane and the other in Orchard Street to hold water from Keycol. The two bore-holes at White Hill provide hard water from the chalk and soft from the greensand. The latter was mixed in larger quantities so when the village was supplied from White Hill we had reputedly the softest water in the country but as the population grew the sources changed and included water from Matts Hill which is the hardest. The Bredhurst reservoir, at the top of Maidstone Road, was built in 1919 to allow land south of the A2 to be developed. Previously each property needed access to a well. The homes of George Mattocks, a water engineer, and George Callaway, a farmer, appear in the lower photograph.

London Road, Rainham, Kent.

London Road

Imagine you are standing underneath the footbridge across the A2 from the Howard School to Bloors Lane. This is the scene you would have witnessed one hundred years ago. The card was posted on October 9th 1912. The house on the right is still recognisable beside the school fence. It was built by Mr Harvey for his own residence. He called it 'Yevrah Dene', his wife's name spelt backwards. Mr Jelly built his home next to the waterworks land at the top of White Hill (now Guardian Court). It is difficult to imagine the busy main A2 London Road could ever have looked like this.

Much easier to recognise is this 1960s view of London Road. Still very little traffic, it might just be possible to take such a picture now. Before Dutch Elm disease ravaged the country in the 1970s the route of the A2 was lined with these magnificent trees. On the left stands the Roman Catholic Church dedicated to St Thomas of Canterbury, which was opened by the Bishop of Southwark in 1958. The original church, built in 1935 and now used as the church hall, is hidden behind.

A very easily recognisable view of the entrance to Rainham showing the Gas Show Rooms and Durrell's Garage on the right. Although there is little traffic in this picture yellow lines have already been painted down the side of the main road with 'slow' in the centre of the carriageway. Maidstone Road and Berengrave Lane formed a crossroads with the A2 until this became too dangerous and traffic to and from Berengrave Lane was diverted along Birling Avenue.

Steady growth from a total of 722 in 1801 meant that by 1900 Rainham had a population of over 3,500 (3,693 at the 1901 census). New homes were required and Century Road is one of the easiest new roads to date correctly. A century later the Millennium Hall was named to commemorate the dawn of the 21st century. As Harvey Road goes off to the right it would seem likely that Marshall Harvey also had a hand in this development.

Holding, Brown and Quinnell Streets formed Gillingham's first Council Estate in Rainham. They were named for former Parish Councillors, Alderman Holding, a farmer and green grocer, Mr Quinnell a grocer and Mr Brown, landlord of the Railway Tavern.

Century Road, Rainham, Kent.

Berengrave Lane

During the 1920s wooden bungalows, often with substantial plots of land, began to spring up along the western side of Berengrave Lane below the railway bridge. Then more permanent houses gradually appeared. One flint bungalow at the top of the lane was listed by the Cyclists' Touring Club as a good stopping place for refreshments. The 'Blue Bowl' later served teas here, but now Hidsons showroom has replaced both. Gone too is the post-war single-storey branch of the Midland Bank, formerly No.1. High Street. Its business was transferred to the new shopping centre in 1987, and the building disappeared not long afterwards.

When this Edwardian photograph was taken the only dwellings along Berengrave Lane were farms. Beyond the railway bridge lay Queen Court, which was occupied by farm bailiff William Few at the time of the 1901 census. Of considerably more importance was Berengrave Farm, where 'Squire' Walter, who was a magistrate to whom ordinary people touched their caps respectfully, farmed 540 acres and employed more than thirty on his land. He and his four daughters lived at Berengrove House, where they were attended by a staff of six - housekeeper, cook, three housemaids and a coachman.

Colonel Day was the resident at Berengrove in the 1920s and 30s. He made the grounds available for Rainham Scouts' Revels in July 1932, but apologised that though he would continue to support the movement, he could no longer act as Scoutmaster. The Sea Scout Headquarters and Rainham's Cricket Club today occupy some of the Berengrove Grounds.

On misty nights lone travellers in the lane might be disturbed by mysterious rustlings and cracklings, then terrified by an unearthly cry. They could not see Colonel Day's old donkey as it wandered through fallen holly leaves in its paddock.

Berengrove House

Cozenton Farm was owned by Lord Hothfield until 1921. Walter Prentis, who lived here at the end of the nineteenth century, farmed 350 acres lying between Bloors Lane and Berengrave Lane, aided by seven men and three boys.

The ancient farmhouse was surrounded by a range of outbuildings including a granary, stables, cattle sheds and an open-fronted cart shed. In this aerial photograph of Cozenton Berengrove House can also be seen amid trees on the right.

When David Richardson and his wife bought Cozenton Farm from Lord Hothfield in 1921 some of the land was orchard, some fields were arable and others supported a small dairy herd. Fish bawleys from Brightlingsea brought mixed catches of sprats, starfish and mussels to Stewart's Wharf to be ploughed into the fields as

fertilizer. They then yielded excellent crops of cabbages and brussels sprouts. Potatoes grown on the farm were sold from clamps beside the footpath at 3/- per hundredweight.

At this period an agricultural labourer's wage was 18-20/- per week.

Opposite Cozenton Farm in the 1930s stood the Berengrave Stores kept by Miss Hunter. When the old barn at the farm caught fire the heat was so great that the sweets in the shop melted. The shop was demolished in the late 1980s to make way for new houses. Much of the former farmland remains 'green', however, since it is now Cozenton Park, and the Council Nurseries at the rear recycle garden waste rather than smelly fish.

Longley's Nurseries

Many will remember Longley's rose gardens which, until the 1970s, lay just below the railway bridge in Berengrave Lane. At one time the gardens stretched between Station Road and Berengrave Lane from the railway line as far as Longley Road. At their peak they attracted visitors (including Lady Elizabeth Bowes-Lyon) from far afield to enjoy the sight and scent of up to 50,000 roses in about 400 varieties.

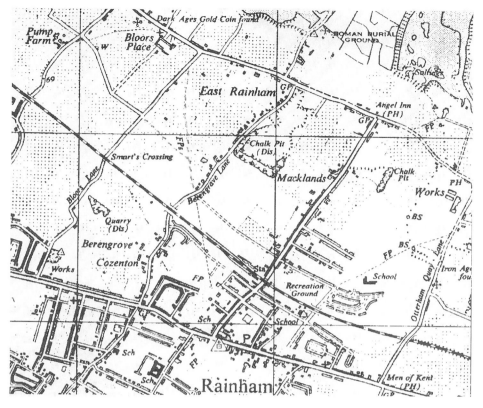

Donald Clarke, who as a boy lived at Pump Farm, recalled his walk home from the School at the top of Station Road in the 1930s through cherry orchards, then along the footpath through the rose gardens, across Berengrave Lane and via what was known as Damson Walk to Cutters Lane. (This walk is still possible, though it now has the unromantic title of 'Bridleway GB 6A')

The Longley family firm of nurserymen also had premises in the High Street near Stratford Lane. Pond House, where it is believed that the Royal Warrant for the supply of roses was proudly displayed, was almost hidden from view by ivy and a large monkey puzzle. Other shrubs and trees were also grown, and in 1912 two notable features were a sequoia over 30' high grown from seed, and a trellis 100' in length covered in wisteria. A royal connection with Queen Mary is certain, for when she visited the Exhibitions held by the National Rose Society she would select those prize-winning arrangements in the 'Basket' class, often won by Longley's, which appealed to her, and expect to receive them as a gift from the grower fortunate enough to have been singled out for her gracious patronage.

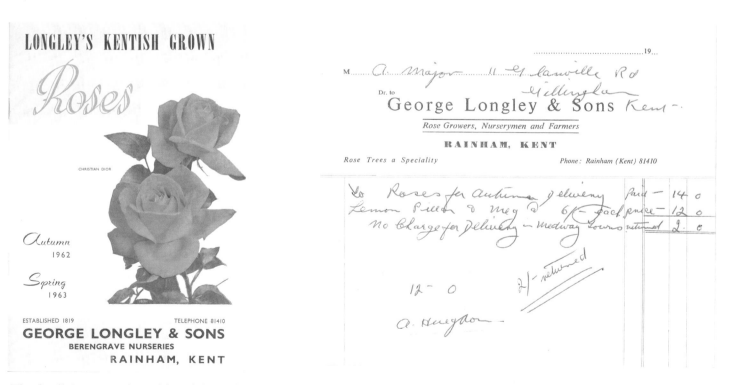

The family's connection with Rainham dates back to 1819. George Longley, who came from Sheldwich, operated a nursery off Chapel Lane (now Mierscourt Road): the two semi-detached houses high above the road opposite Cherry Tree Road still bear the name 'Nursery Cottages'. Six acres of this land, known as Mardel Field, were once planted with cherry trees.

The Gas Show Rooms

Gas, supplied by The Rochester, Chatham & Gillingham Gas Company, first came to Rainham on February 24th 1868. This was a momentous occasion as an illuminated star was exhibited at the White Horse. This encouraged the village to raise the necessary funds for street lighting, from Orchard Street to High Dewar Road and down to the railway station, and to heat and light the church. This was accomplished by Christmas Eve 1869 when the lamp lighter Henry Honey entered his duties for the first time. By Palm Sunday April 10th 1870 the church was also supplied and a special evening service was held at seven o'clock to celebrate the event.

In 1926 this imposing Gas Show Room was built. Until it closed in 1979 it was quite an experience paying a gas bill in the spacious display area set out with all the latest appliances. In December 1932 a pedestrian crossing the London Road was fatally injured when a motorist failed to see her. The cause of the accident was partially attributed to the flood lighting in front of the showrooms. In the jury's opinion these lights had a disturbing influence on drivers in the roadway! The flat above the show rooms provided an elegant home for the manager. Miss Margaret List had very fond memories of the twenty years that her family spent in this home whilst her father had responsibility for the show rooms and the gas supply to Rainham. She was horrified, as were many other locals, when in 2003 the present owners gave 'Manor Farm' a facelift and quite changed its appearance.

Alderman William Holding

Alderman William Holding lived in the white wooden building at the corner of Holding Street, now an Estate Agents, which was once the farmhouse for Street Farm. He later built a house on the opposite side of the main road called 'Wilelda' (a combination of his own name with his wife Chriselda). He then converted the wooden building to a greengrocers shop and another small part of the same building became a sweet shop run by Mrs B. Kitchingham who was the daughter of Mr Halrose, whose own sweet shop was on the banks in the High Street opposite Ivy Street. Barbara Kitchingham also became a well known local dignitary serving for many years on Gillingham Council.

Alderman Holding and his son at a street party in Holding Street to celebrate VJ Day (Victory in Japan) in August 1945. Mr Holding served for many years on the council and Holding Street, which was built in the 1930s, was named in his honour as one of the first elected councillors on the new 1929 Gillingham Council.

Amy Johnson

Amy Johnson (1904 –1941) was a British aviator who obtained fame after she made the first solo flight from Britain to Australia in nine and a half days in 1930. She subsequently toured the country and here a small crowd has gathered to see her drive through Rainham. The Kent Messenger of 4th July 1936 reported that Amy Mollison (Johnson) arrived at Rochester Airport, drove to the Mayor of Rochester's parlour for civic greetings, then on to Rainham where there were 'large crowds in the streets' and back to the Central Hotel for a civic lunch'.

(Facts did not stand in the way of a good story even then it would appear.)

The land behind the wall, opposite Lloyds bank, stood empty for many years after the demolition of the cottages, but is now the site of Ashurst Place. Dick the road man lived in one of the cottages and loved to sit in his front garden chatting to the passers by. The row of houses, from Orchard Street, was built in two stages, the smaller ones on the left being constructed first in about 1904. These have been renovated and are again occupied as homes. One of the posters on the side of the house is advertising a cherry tree auction. This was a common practice, any interested party could buy the fruit a few weeks before it would be ready to pick. Thus the buyer took the risk of a late frost or heavy rainstorm ruining the crop. It was a gamble, some years it was possible to make a fortune but it was equally likely the crop would be a complete failure.

Coningsby House

Coningsby House, 69 High Street, stood almost opposite Orchard Street, one of the now forgotten houses of Rainham. According to the 1891 census Mr Coningsby lived in this house, hence the name. By 1952 the house was owned by Mr Reginald Oswick who occupied the ground floor with his wife and son. The upper floor had been let since their marriage in 1949 to Bill and Joyce Atkinson. It was a beautiful old house with a very large entrance hall. The upstairs kitchen had a fireplace so large you could walk into it and the house had a charming walled garden.

The Bargain House

The Bargain House came to Rainham in 1924 taking a site previously occupied by G.Hooker. Mr Bays expanded his business having opened in Burnt Oak Terrace, Gillingham in 1910.

The Bargain House was quite a feature in Rainham having a prominent position in the centre of the village. The corrugated iron roof was far from attractive but it was one of the most useful places. The shop stocked a whole range of hardware. One Rainham girl, Miss Betty Fullager, started working at the shop at the top of Station Road on leaving school in 1926 aged 14 years. She stayed with the same business all her working life, transferring to Gillingham

when the Bargain House closed and only retiring from the King Street shop, now run by Mr Bays' grandson Jonathan Baynes, in the late 1970s. The shop prospered in Rainham only closing when the high street plots and a small part of the school playground were purchased by Barclays Bank for their grand new building in 1936.

Rainham Cinema

The original Rainham Cinema was in a large hut built of tin and wood near where the United Services Club now stands. In those early days of silent films Mrs Sayer, a local pianist, valiantly fitted her music to the tempo of the film, often having to improvise when the film broke or the projector failed. Children filled this hut each Saturday for 1d or 2d a seat and the rest paid 4d or 6d for the evening shows. It was in this building

that the Rainham Fire Brigade would have organised its Cinematograph Entertainments in 1917. Later the hall occupied by the Salvation Army in the High Street was adapted to become 'The Royal Cinema' (colloquially known as 'The Bughutch') after a new Citadel was built in Station Road. The cinema closed in March 1966 sadly lamented by courting couples who greatly enjoyed the double seats at the back of the auditorium. The building was then used by Vyes the Kentish Grocers who were subsequently taken over by Liptons and when they closed the building was acquired by Lukehursts who still trade there as a furniture store.

Trams

The original 1906 tram terminus in Rainham was in the High Street at the top of Station Road. Here the conductor disconnected the power arm from the overhead cables and swung it round 180 degrees to reconnect for the journey back to Chatham whilst the driver simply walked to the other end of the tram. The obvious inconvenience to other traffic meant that the terminus was very soon moved a few yards around the corner into Station Road. This was bad news for passengers who left things a bit late. From the High Street the conductor had been able see them rushing up the road and hold the tram for them: now they had to get up a bit earlier!

The Cricketers

One of the biggest changes in the centre of Rainham was in the 1930s when the new Cricketers Public House was constructed behind the old building. The old Inn was demolished leaving a small courtyard in front. This is the closest Rainham comes to possessing a 'village green' or open public space and in recent years fulfils this purpose as youngsters fill the benches and tables relaxing and enjoying a drink on warm summer evenings. In 1925 the East Kent Gazette reported that Rainham Parish Council had agreed to pay a rent of £1 per annum for the piece of ground belonging to the Cricketers Public House on which a public convenience was to be erected. This was still in use until the late 1970s when the new shopping centre was built including public conveniences.

St Margaret's Parish Church

The parish of Rainham was in the diocese of Canterbury until November 1938 when it was transferred to Rochester. This followed the incorporation of Rainham into the Borough of Gillingham in 1929 whereas we had previously been part of Milton Rural District. At the same time we transferred from the Faversham Parliamentary Constituency to Gillingham. Thus our removal from East Kent to West was complete. This made economic and social sense to the powers that be but did not please the residents of Rainham. As a small concession Rainham railway station was allowed to keep its name and we were saved the indignity of becoming 'Gillingham East'.

Rainham Church and War Memorial.

A church in Rainham is first mentioned in a document written circa 1100, though it is very likely that a church existed before the Norman Conquest. In 1137 Robert de Crevecoeur gave the canons of the priory he had founded at Leeds the right to nominate the vicar of Rainham and he also donated 18 acres of land in the village. There are a few remains of the Norman church in the east wall of the chancel, but the building is almost entirely of Gothic design. 13th century Early English style can be seen in the chancel, the 'Decorated' 14th century period may be seen in the nave and the 'Perpendicular' 15th century period of Gothic architecture is visible in the tower.

The church is constructed of Kentish ragstone and flint with a tiled roof. Extensive repairs have been undertaken at regular intervals particularly in the 1860s and 70s when the dormer windows in the south roof were removed and the north porch rebuilt in Victorian style. Much essential work continues to this day at ever increasing cost to the parish.

One of the most striking features of the church is the ceiling painting at the east end of the nave. The celure or canopy was erected by Sir Thomas St Leger of Siloam, a manor on the eastern edge of Rainham, in the 15th century. The sun-in-splendour design was the badge of the then Yorkist King Edward IV whose sister Anne was married to Sir Thomas. Edward was succeeded by Richard III but following his death it was thought wise to add red petals and convert the white rose to the new Tudor emblem. The celure, which has recently been restored during the work on the roof in 2009, was built as a canopy of honour for a rood screen that stretched across the whole width of the building but has long since disappeared.

When the font was being moved in the early 1980s it was discovered that another vault lay beneath the north west end of the nave in addition to the two known vaults beneath the Tufton chapel. One of the Tufton vaults houses the church heating system whilst the other contains 43 coffins belonging to members of the Tufton family. The Tuftons succeeded the Bloors, who as leading landowners in Rainham gave their name to Bloors Place. Sir Christopher Bloor was the last of the line but his daughter, Olympia, married Sir John Tufton of Hothfield, near Ashford, during the reign of Elizabeth I. The vault of Hothfield church was prone to flooding. Because of this in the 17th century the bodies of Sir John and Olympia were transferred to Rainham and thereafter many members of the family were buried at Rainham. The newly discovered vault contained two coffins, one belonging to the Russell family of Greenwich who are believed to have built the vault. The other bears the inscription 'MRS IOSEIA MARIA AVGED DELOOR USSELL died August 25th 1735 aged 28 years'.

St Margaret's Choir

This photograph of St Margaret's Church Choir in the early 1920s was taken in the Vicarage garden looking towards Station Road.

Back row: F. Wickens, A. Lockyer, W.A. Cooke, A. Manktelow, J. Dennis, A. Copsey, Lamb, Flood, ?

Third row: J. Coomber (Churchwarden) G. Nichols, K.J. Oldland, F.G. Seager, G. Bone Snr, W.A.R. Ball (Vicar), J. Cornford Snr, J. Cornford, R. Ockwell, S. Norris, P. Edmonds (Churchwarden).

Second row: G. Wickins, G. Foster, D. Oldland, W.G. Thomas, G.R. Bone (Organist & Choirmaster) F. Ockwell, B. Foster, R. Oldland, R. Cresser, M. Wickins.

Front row: H. Bell, H. Kitchingham, A. Deed, L. Garlinge, E. Nicholls, T. Taylor, W. Brockman, H. Thomas, Harvey.

In 1908 Mr Bone the organist employed choir boys who could not sing or naughty boys from school (where he was headmaster) to pump the organ. The boys at this time received a farthing for each of the twice weekly choir practices and a halfpenny for each service they attended.

The Church Army

The Church Army is a religious organisation within the Church of England founded in 1882 by Wilson Carlile, an industrialist converted after the failure of his textile firm, who took holy orders in 1880. Originally intended for evangelical and social work in the London slums, it developed along Salvation Army lines and has done much work among ex-prisoners and for the soldiers of both world wars. Church Army members toured villages with their wagon converting many to their cause. This picture was taken whilst visiting Rainham in 1907.

Toc H

Toc H is an interdenominational Christian fellowship open to anyone over the age of 16 and devoted to social service. It was founded in 1915 at Poperinge in Belgium by the Rev P.B. (Tubby) Clayton, a Church of England chaplain, as a military chapel and club. It was named Talbot House in memory of Gilbert Talbot, a British lieutenant killed in action, who was a member of a prominent Anglican family. Its name derives from army signallers' designations of the initials T. H. The motto of 'Abandon rank all ye who enter here' meant each member was given a nickname and all were considered equal at Toc H events. The vicar therefore did not wear his dog collar badge of office and Army Officers and other ranks were of equal standing. Many of the Toc H nicknames stuck to their owners for life.

Back row: Springate, Foulsham, Greenwood, Raines, Parker, Horton, Springate, Monk, ?

Front row: Sargeant, Bartlett, Rev Hodgson, Bert Newell, G.K. Turner, C.R. Wakeley. ?.

1st Rainham Guides

The Officers, Patrol Leaders and Patrol Seconders of 1st Rainham Guides probably taken in the late 1930s. Guides had been founded in Rainham in 1919 by Miss Marion Tritton – Captain, a teacher at the Council school, with Miss Florence Tuft (later Mrs Rayner) as her lieutenant. Miss Doris Johnson joined the company in 1920 and became lieutenant when Miss Tuft married. Her sister Tess Johnson took over as Captain when Miss Tritton became Mrs Wickens in 1923. The two Johnsons ran the company – with sister Miss Elsie as Brown Owl helped by youngest sister Poppy and with sister Linda as Instructress until Tess, seen here in the centre, married Victor Ballard in 1940. Mrs Rayner started Rangers and with Miss P Game ran the company for many years. Mrs Rayner was mainly responsible for the dramatic work performed by Guides, Rangers and St Margaret's Players.

Church of England School

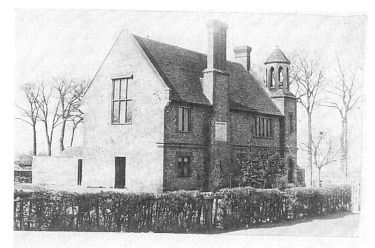

For 130 years one of the most commanding sites in Rainham was the Church of England School which stood at the top of Station Road. It is said that the original school began in the south porch of the church but there is little evidence to support this claim. However by 1838 there was a National School in the High Street, probably near the Post Office as John Vinter was both schoolmaster and postmaster. By 1846 a new National School built with money donated by landowners and public subscription (£685 7s 3d) was built on the corner of Station Road and the High Street. It was opened by the curate Rev F.F. Haslewood, and Mr Vinter, then 74 years old, was allowed to retire with a small pension. A small National School was opened in Lower Rainham in 1876. In 1878 the building was enlarged to the north and what became the boys' school was added, and as Rainham continued to grow in 1884 a further extension was built this time to the

south where an infants department was created. The Headmaster's quarters were adapted for the Girls' School and the lower schoolroom became Rainham's first Church Hall. The pictures show the three stages of the building programme. The large elm tree by the fence of the playground provided welcome shade for the children in summer. The iron staircases were added when it was considered the steps inside were unsuitable for children, first a staircase at the back but as fire risks were considered another set was built at the front. This is how many will remember the school as it remained like this until it was demolished in 1977 to make way for the new shopping centre. The last ten years of its life saw rapid decline after the school moved out to Orchard Street and it was used as a temporary community centre whilst the Station Oasts were converted.

The field behind the school was used for many parish gatherings. It was here that the celebrations for King George V's coronation were held on June 23rd 1911. Each child was presented with a coronation mug. Mrs Helena Thomas, who was two years old at the time, remembers with regret to this day immediately hurling hers at her brother and breaking it because as a schoolchild he had been given a bigger mug.

Part of this field was later acquired by the education committee to provide plots for the boys for gardening lessons.

Rainham Boys School Cricket Team in 1930.
Back row: Albert Gowers, Fred Briggs, Mr G.K. Turner, Bill Edwards, Ted Wickenden,
Middle row: Percy Morris, Cliff Warner, Harry Howting, Sid Blundy, Ted Oliver.
Front row: Harry Wickenden, Phil (Freddie) Cooper.

TRAM TERMINUS, RAINHAM, KENT.

Trams

A series of photographs was taken to celebrate the arrival of the first tram in Rainham in 1906. The picture shows the crowd, dressed in their Sunday best, including many children drawn to the occasion. Several of the pictures include the old Cricketers Inn, the row of shops that still stand to the right of the pub and the newly constructed houses beyond Orchard Street.

The tram faced little competition from other road traffic in 1906 so the waiting crowd had no fear standing in the road.

War Memorial

The War Memorial, a replica of the Cross of Iona, was dedicated on December 12th 1920. This photograph probably taken very soon after that event shows the original iron railings which surrounded the memorial. These were removed in 1940 during the patriotic appeals of the Second World War, supposedly for use in the rearmament of the country. Rumour had it that much of this salvaged iron was dumped as unsuitable for use in the arms trade but the drive continued in order to focus the minds of the population on the perilous state of the country. The railings have never been replaced and the scars where they were removed may still be seen on the low wall surrounding the cross.

In July 1940 Lord Beaverbrook's request for aluminium for 'Pots for Planes' met with an enthusiastic response in Rainham. Miss Quinnell loaned a High Street shop to the WVS as a collection point. Everyone contributed and the Rainham Guides and Rangers made door to door collections. The result was two large lorry loads which were speedily despatched.

Tram Terminus, Rainham.

V.E. Day

By May 1945 when this VE Day procession was pictured the old Cricketers had gone and the new building stands in its place. The two flag bearers are Ronald Williamson and Brian Touchner with Mr and Mrs Clohessey on the right in the foreground, their daughter Anita on the tricycle, Mrs Freeman, her daughter Mary and Mrs Wilkinson centre front and Mrs Gilberthorpe and son Peter and Mrs Clouhew centre back.

The White Horse

The White Horse was one of four public houses listed in Rainham in Pigot's 1839 Directory. The other three were The Cricketers, The Green Lion and The George & Dragon. By the 1870s The White Horse boasted 'very fine livery stables', and it was the Liberal Party's headquarters during the election of 1874. This picture shows the newly rebuilt White Horse in about 1900 after the disastrous fire of 1892. For many years it was run by Charles Adie, assisted by his sons. By the mid 1930s there were garages rather than stables, and aviaries to attract visitors who called for lunch or tea.

The chestnut trees opposite are reputed to have been planted by Charles Adie's predecessor, Mr Sayer, to commemorate the birth of each of his children.

Church House

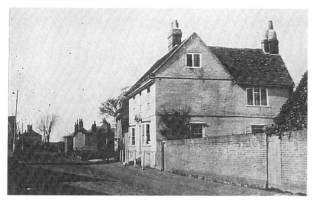 

Church House, which stood beside the White Horse, was occupied at the end of the nineteenth century by the Misses Dodd. Their earlier home had been Cozenton Farm, which had been run by their widowed mother Emma with the help of a farm bailiff. They had been educated by a governess, an advantage very few in Rainham enjoyed.

As one of many ways of raising money to buy a Spitfire, in November 1940 a display of 'donations by the Germans' was held at Church House. This exhibition, which ultimately raised over £20, included parts of unexploded bombs, flares and weapons, and relics from a Dornier plane which had crashed at Victoria Station. A month later it was decided to make the house a Club Centre for forces personnel in the area. Donations and volunteers to help serve refreshments were sought by the Committee, which included many of Rainham's better-known residents - the Vicar, (Mr Maples Earl), Colonel Iremonger, Alderman Holding and Miss Quinnell. The palm tree now in the grounds of Rainham's new Healthy Living Centre grew in the garden of Church House.

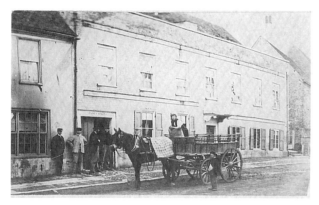

Marlborough House

This was the home of maltster James Atkins and family in 1841. One of his daughters, Laura, was a governess, while in a single-storey brick building to the rear her sister Bertha ran a small school for young children. By the 1930s Mr and Mrs Game and their four daughters occupied the house. They took in 'guests' such as school teachers, so that the house acted as a rather superior boarding house. Meanwhile the building abutting on to Church Path was reopened as Marlborough House School by Miss Muriel Flood and Miss Joy Bolton. Here the forty or so pupils learned thoughtfulness and good manners as well as ordinary lessons, and although some children left for Grammar School at about the age of eleven, others stayed until they were fourteen. It was much loved by those who attended and there were many regrets when it had to close in 1938 following the death of Mr Game and the sale of Marlborough House. In 1939 an ARP Control Room and Police station were set up here, covering an area stretching from the Central Hotel on the A2 (at the top of Featherby Road) to the eastern outskirts of Rainham, and from Bloors Place south to Hempstead. This necessitated the installation of four telephones, two for outgoing and two for incoming calls. The Control Room later moved to Durland House.

The Green Lion

Research following the discovery of a Sun Alliance firemark dated 1790 showed that the victualler then was Peter Hard, and that the building and its contents were insured for £400. A study of the roof timbers has established that this building was a medieval hall house dating back to the 14th century. In the 17th century a new floor was created internally, and dormer windows were inserted in the roof. The house was encased in brick and chimneys built on to the external walls. The whole building was refronted in the Georgian era, as was The Cricketers, when coaches using the newly turnpiked road brought prosperity to Rainham's inns. During renovations in the 1970s a concealed room was found in the roof, perhaps used as a hiding place from authority. Legend has a highwayman named Dick Shepherd visiting the inn, but different versions have him captured and hanged near the top of Berengrave Lane, or alternatively escaping by jumping through a window. Does the Lion have a ghost? One guest reported seeing a 'lady' in his room, and rooms on the top floor had a creepy feel... What is fact is the tunnel which once led from the cellars to the church, found during construction of the new Marlborough House.

Like other public houses it was home to benefit societies such as the Ancient Order of Foresters. During the 1930s the Landlord was Phil Curling, and the pub was a centre for sportsmen. Mr Curling himself acted as handicapper for all kinds of events. The bowling green which lay behind the house was dug up to grow vegetables during the war years.

The Vicarage

The Vicarage was built in the reign of Queen Elizabeth I to replace the Parsonage (see page 3) but by the late 1950s such a large house was a burden on the parish for upkeep and maintenance. The valuable site in the High Street was therefore sold and a new smaller modern Vicarage constructed in Broadview Avenue. During the move it was rumoured that many of the parish records and documents were unceremoniously thrown down the disused well and so lost forever.

The site, next to Rainham Post Office, was developed as the local sorting office with space left in front for a new Post Office building. This never materialised and eventually the sorting office was demolished in 2003 and Appletree Court, a McCarthy & Stone retirement development, now occupies the land.

Rainham High Street

The door on the left in the centre of the photograph was that of the London and Provincial Bank, whose premises these were from at least 1908. The London and Provincial was absorbed by Barclays in the 1930s and shortly afterwards its activities were transferred to a fine new building at the top of Station Road. The shop next door, with blinds, was a drapers and milliners, while the other neighbour was Cattermole the jeweller. Then came Rainham's Post Office, which after a century is still trading from the same building. Now it is combined with a convenience store: in 1908 the Post Office and Telephone Exchange was run by Arthur Cozens in conjunction with his business as stationer and photographer.

By the 1930s traffic had become a severe problem through Rainham High Street, although it would not appear so from this picture. Regularly on fine summer Sundays coaches and cars would queue for miles along the A2. Even at other times it could be almost impossible to cross the road. The Cheeseman family, at that time, lived in their shoe shop at 112 High Street (see opposite). When the traffic was bad if they wished to post a letter the only safe way was to walk up to the pedestrian crossing by The Cricketers, where there was always a policeman on duty, cross with his help, run down to the letterbox by the Post Office and return the same way. On one occasion one sister decided to try and dodge the traffic and avoid this unnecessary walk but she was caught by a car and suffered severe lacerations to her leg. Dr Irby Webster was called and sewed up her wounds by candlelight, the only means of artificial light above ground floor. The East Kent Gazette newspaper reported in September 1932 of 'Troublesome Road Reconstruction. Owing to the reconstruction of the road in Rainham High Street, considerable disorganisation of the traffic was caused on Sunday evening. It was only possible for cars to proceed one way, and during the rush hours, blocks of traffic extended to as far as Hartlip Hill. Here were also several minor accidents caused by bumping as cars came to a standstill.' The problems continued after the war until the construction of the M2 in 1962 relieved the towns of much of the coastal traffic.

Barling's Drapery Stores

W. H. BARLING'S DRAPERY STORES, RAINHAM.

W.H. Barling continued the business previously owned by Walter Rush in 'Manchester House' on the corner of Ivy Street, most recently, until November 2009, occupied by Age Concern. A 1908 advertisement for the shop declares they have: 'Up-to-date drapery and goods of every description, special attention given to millinery, a splendid selection of dress materials and curtains' plus they are 'Agents for Frister & Rossmann's Sewing Machines and Mortimer Brothers' and finally they are agents for 'High class dyers and cleaners'.

Coronation 1953

Rainham 'en fete' for the Coronation celebrations in 1953. Unfortunately after months of planning the actual day was an almost complete wash out and several events had to be either postponed or cancelled. A permanent memorial is the clock over Barclays Bank which was presented to Rainham by the committee who organised the celebrations. Many hours of deliberation finally concluded that this would be a good use for the money left over after the event. A small plaque on the wall commemorates this. The Borough guaranteed to maintain and repair the clock, an arrangement that continued until 2009.

Stratford Lane may just be seen at the front left of this picture. In May 1940 an air raid exercise was carried out using Mr Scott's Oasts at Stratford Lane. These were deemed to be a department store

High Street, Rainham, Kent

hit by a high explosive bomb. Many casualties were supposedly trapped in the upper storeys (the volunteers included some truanting schoolboys). Smoke from flares simulated a realistic effect but the experience fortunately never had to be repeated for real in Rainham.

112 High Street

A view from the top deck of a bus taken in the 1960s. The shop on the right (112 High Street) is part of a very old building possibly constructed by the monks of Leeds Abbey as a hostel for themselves whilst building St Margaret's Church. A magnificent king post supported the roof and the building had a preservation order. Unfortunately after it had remained empty for some time it was found that the king post had been removed and the structure was in a very dangerous condition. Demolition was considered to be the only option. The site is now part of Hidsons open display area.

Tasmania House

This house, in Pudding Road, is said to have been built by a man who had made his fortune as a settler in Australia. For many years it was the home of the Callaway family. George Callaway, a horse-dealer who established a market garden in Pudding Road at the beginning of the twentieth century, had four sons and by hard work they managed to acquire Platters Farm which was mostly rough fields and woodland. With the rapid development of the south of Rainham in the 1950s this land became very valuable and much of the farm was sold by Mr Sidney Callaway for housing, the field beside the A2 being reserved for the two new secondary schools. Although now a wealthy man it made no difference to Sidney - he 'never knew how to spend his money'. In fact he was a generous donor to several local causes: Rainham Cricket Club and Gillingham FC were two beneficiaries. He also gave the church the land on which the Millennium Hall now stands, and donated money for repair of the church tower.

The origin of the name 'Pudding Road' is uncertain, but one suggestion is that it indicated the type of soil found there.

The road once had its own beerhouse, 'The Woodman', whose landlord was Jock 'Snuffers' Mackenzie. It closed in about 1910, and now forms two private houses.

Edwin Jelly

It was Mr Jelly as a Director and Vice-Chairman of the Rainham Land Company who was responsible for much of Rainham's development during the early years of the last century, giving his name to Edwin Road. Originally from Somerset, he first managed a clothier's shop on the Banks which he later purchased, then opened this larger 'Clothing, Hat and Boot Stores' on the opposite side of the High Street. He was one of the prime movers in obtaining the Recreation Ground as a public amenity. His premises later became The Colour Shop, the source of paint, wallpaper and other decorating needs before the advent of enormous DIY centres. Today Hon's Chinese Restaurant occupies the building.

The Chestnuts

This building, which now forms an integral part of the sheltered housing complex known as Longford Court, was formerly the home of Lt.Col.Godby, but by 1935 it had become the house and surgery of Dr Longford. As can be seen from the photographs, there was once an extension to the west (the section to the right of the drainpipe) spoiling the symmetrical appearance.

Belmont House 110 High Street. (Left, now the site of Hidson's Show Rooms) Between the two world wars this was the home of Mrs Knight, widower of Mr Knight, manager of Wakeley's brick field. During the second world war the house was used as a hostel for Wrens and later for homeless families. It was built as a religious house at the same time as the church and 112 High Street by the monks of Leeds Abbey.

Durland House (Right) Like the Green Lion this building is much older than its facade suggests. It was originally timber-framed, but during the 17th century another storey was added and the whole building was encased in brick. It is now a retirement home. The census of 1901 records Caroline Thurlow as its occupier, together with her two daughters and a boarder, all dressmakers.

East end of High Street

On the extreme left of this view, dating from the 1950s, can be seen Gilbert's ladder-making workshop. Mr Gilbert was also an undertaker. In later years this lean-to building was used as a paper store for Jenwoods, the printers. On the opposite side of the street the trees on each side of The Chestnuts now dwarf the house. Plans to fell one of them in 1939, which would have involved diverting traffic for two or three days, were presumably deferred because of the outbreak of war.

Russells

A little further along the street towards Sittingbourne was the home of the Quinnell family, 'Russells', once a farmhouse. They owned numerous properties throughout Rainham, their grocery business (next to The Lion) having prospered. George Quinnell had six children, all of whom at some time worked in the business, and later were noted for their social work in the village. By the time this picture was taken they could afford to enjoy some relaxation in their garden, which ran down to the school in Solomon Road and contained a large rabbit warren. The garden was tended by a gardener who occupied Russells Cottage next door. The family also kept two indoor servants. In the 18th century Edward Hasted described 'Russells' as a neat modern house belonging to John Russell of Greenwich. The site is now occupied by Sutton Close and part of Scott Avenue.

Congregational Church

The building seen here was erected in 1891 when the congregation outgrew its first chapel at the bottom of Chapel Lane (now called Mierscourt Road). This had been founded with the help of the Chatham Ebenezer Meeting, who provided the first preachers, and it remained in use for the Sunday School, (and for wedding receptions and other social functions) until 1964, when the cost of maintenance became too great and it was sold to the Borough Council. The new chapel, seen here, had sittings for 300, and possessed a good organ. Sunday services were held at 10.45 and 6.30 in 1909, when the Pastor was Mr E.S. Wilkinson. By the 1920s there was a flourishing football team, which won the Free Church Second Division Championship in the 1922/3 season.

Though unchanged in outward appearance the church gained a new title in 1972 when Congregationalists and Presbyterians combined to become the United Reformed Church. But the numbers attending dwindled until, only twenty years later, the church closed and the building was bought and converted for use as an advertising agency by Pentad. Their tenure was short, and it is now the home of ISP, an organisation concerned with children's welfare. Only one of the adjacent cottages was still occupied in 1969, and they have since been demolished.

The Rose Public House

This hostelry has supplied liquid refreshment to the public since at least 1870, and is now noted for its food. The beers advertised in the 1930s were 'Masons Maidstone Prize Ales'; Shepherd Neame is the brewery today. Confusingly Rainham in 1939 also had licensed premises called 'The Rosebud', situated in Ivy Street. At different times at least two other beerhouses existed in this area, the Walnut Tree near Stratford Lane and the Pear Tree near the top of Otterham Quay Lane. These small alehouses acted as local community centres, where the men could escape from their often crowded cottages for relaxation over a drink with friends.

The Rose stands at the corner of the road whose name has taken various forms over

RAINHAM BROADWALK

the years. Currently 'High Dewar Road' it was listed as 'Hydore Lane' (also called Drury lane) in Kelly's Directory of 1908, and other spellings include 'Dory', 'Idore' and 'Hi Dore'.

WAKELEY RD. RAINHAM.

Wakeley Road

There are new houses now where once these trees separated the unsurfaced road from the Recreation Ground. On the left hand side, near the junction with Station Road, was William Higgins' Woodyard, adjacent to his house, Tugela Villa. Higgins specialised in fencing and supplied spiles - stakes, not a misprint for stiles.

The three roads William Street, Henry Street and Wakeley Road were named for Mrs William Henry Wakeley, Chairman of the Rainham Land Company.

Rainham Pottery

This mock Tudor cottage, on the A2 at Broad Walk, was in use as a showroom for Upchurch Pottery by 1929, but it had originally been built by the Wakeley family as a convalescent home for their consumptive son. The history of the Upchurch and Rainham Potteries is short but interesting: they were two independent businesses but the potters came from the same family, the Bakers.

Upchurch Pottery was financed by Mrs Seymour Wakeley, the potter was Edward James Baker who had wide experience of the trade,

and wanted to run his own business. In 1913 a bottle kiln and workshop were erected in the chalkpit in Seymour Road (then known as Wakeley's Lane) owned by the Wakeleys. Mr Baker and two of his sons, Ted and James, gained a good reputation for their work, particularly the large pots and the subtle glazes they produced, despite the primitive conditions - water came

from a pond and paraffin lamps were used for illumination. But in 1935, because the pottery was not very profitable, Mrs Wakeley leased it briefly to Mr and Mrs Davies, then sold it to Mrs Alice Winnicott. She had some original ideas, but did not always appreciate the practical difficulties involved, which Mr Baker tried to explain. The goods produced during this time of mixed management were given the name 'Claverdon' ware rather than 'Upchurch'.

Meanwhile Mr and Mrs Davies had bought the thatched building from the Wakeleys in 1936, turning it into the Tudor Cafe. Two years later they acquired the adjoining cottage and converted it into a pottery. Ted Baker, like his father, wanted his own business, and so moved here to run the Rainham Pottery, while his elder brother William returned from London to join his father and James at Upchurch. After Mr Baker Senior retired the gradual deterioration of the buildings and vandalism forced the Upchurch Pottery to close. Not long afterwards it was demolished and the chalk pit became a landfill site.

But the Rainham Pottery flourished and its pre-war products, named 'Roeginga' after the Roman name for Rainham, were sold at the Tudor Cafe. The pottery was shut during the war while Ted Baker served in the forces, but after a short period when it and the cafe were leased to a Mr Wilson in 1945, Ted became the pottery's owner, installing electric kilns and employing his brother William and several young women. The firm became famous for its 'Rainham Blue' products, while a new bronze glaze aroused specialist interest. A sign outside the cafe to attract day trippers en route for the Kent coast read 'Come and have a tasty meal, and see the potter at his wheel', for although the cafe and the pottery were separate businesses, they worked together to their mutual benefit. Commemorative items were in demand, and many homes still cherish these, especially since the pottery had to close following Ted's retirement in 1975.

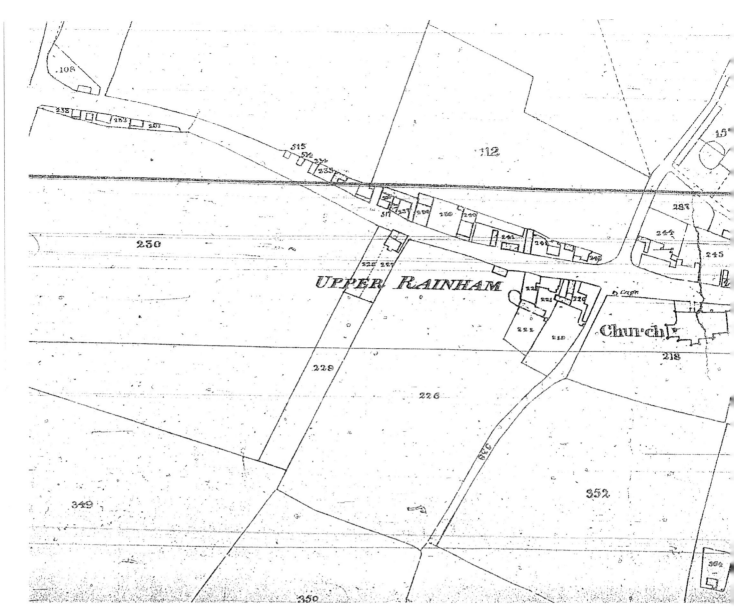

Tithe Map

In the 1840s Upper Rainham comprised scarcely more than the High Street, where the larger houses of the 'gentry' stood cheek by jowl with the cottages occupied by those who served them, and the shops and businesses which catered for all classes. Some buildings shown here are still standing, notably the Church, the Old Parsonage (286) and the Green Lion (210). So too is the row of small cottages which stands at an angle to the A2 near the end of Mierscourt Road. They once faced a pond: the L-shaped part was a malthouse. Close by were the village post office run by John Vinten, and a school for boys (the Girls' National School was at the opposite end of the street). Much of the land to the north was still fields and meadows.

Church Chest

The 14th century oak church chest is a particularly fine example. It is carved with two tiers of tracery and was once painted with red ochre. It was the original storage place for the parish records and could be opened only when all three key holders (the vicar and two churchwardens) were present. The archives are now in the Medway offices at Strood. This picture was probably taken when the chest was restored in 1908/9, by Harris & Sons of Exeter. Its permanent home is the Tufton chapel.

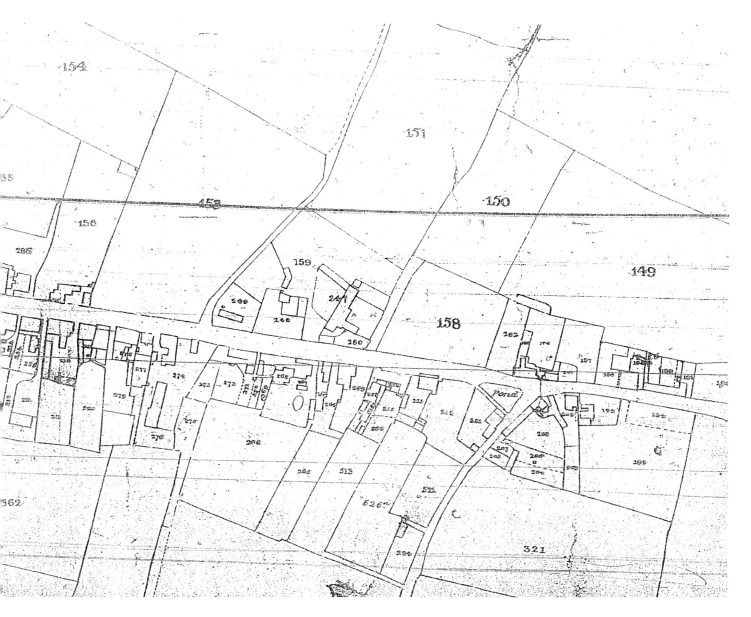

The 'cage' where malefactors were allowed to cool their heels is shown on the edge of the road outside the Church, opposite what is now Station Road. Both the White Horse and The Cricketers were already in business at the junction, but each has been rebuilt in a slightly different position.

A funeral procession with a north view of St Margaret's Church in 1797.

St Margaret's Church and Lockup 1834

Men of Kent

This licensed house, which closed in 2009, first appears in the 1861 census, with James and Sarah Brooker as the occupants. It was named for those born east of the Medway (or perhaps east of a boundary passing through Rainham Mark). Recently the sign has featured two men, one recognisably Charles Dickens, the other anonymous. There was formerly a skittle alley attached to the house, later converted to a tea-room. The Tudor Cafe next door offered an alternative venue for refreshments, so the pub was a favourite pull-in for coaches travelling to and from the Thanet coast before the M2 was opened. As well as serving coach parties it catered for local customers: a child from the nearby

cottages would be sent with a jug to fetch porter for the family. Mine host from 1906 to 1914 was Moses Barden, who was assisted by his daughters.

A hop garden just opposite was a scene of excitement during the war when a German pilot was captured there. Children collecting shrapnel spotted the parachute descending, and they and their mothers watched as the airman, offering no resistance, was surrounded by pole-pullers and arrested.

These small houses to the right in the photograph, whose rents were devoted to 'the poor of Rainham', were called Almshouse Cottages, while Meresborough Road was once known as Almshouse Lane, (sometimes East Kent Lane).

Parish Boundary

The boundary of the parish of Rainham in this area has changed little over the years. The milestone may have been one of the boundary markers that was beaten on the annual 'beating the bounds' walk around the parish. This was an essential practice to teach and remind the inhabitants of the extent of their land. The directions were detailed and precise but could only be followed if updated annually as they included such phrases as 'continue to the bent elm at the southern corner of the field'. This makes it all but impossible to follow the instructions today. Only one of the metal plates remains on the milestone, announcing that the oasthouses stand five miles from Sittingbourne. This is the point at which 'Medway' officially ends, and the postcode changes from ME8 to ME9.

Oasthouses

Originally oasthouses were simply rectangular buildings divided into three sections, with a furnace for drying hops at the centre. Square kilns first appeared in the later eighteenth century, circular ones a generation or so later. The belief that these were more efficient proved false, so by the end of the nineteenth century square kilns, now somewhat larger, reappeared. Almost opposite the oasts as one approaches from Sittingbourne, the first house in Rainham stands at the corner of South Bush Lane. It was built by Lord Hothfield, who owned much of the land and property in the village, to house his agent.

Moor Street

Moor Street House possesses the only remaining mounting block in Rainham. Once there was a bell-cote on the roof, whose bell, like those on the bell-masts at the Dockyard, called men to work. Features like these illustrate the way of life of the wealthy landed gentry in rural Kent in the 18th century.

Rainham was still largely rural in the 1930s. Apart from fruit and hop-growing, sheep were grazed. A Kent Messenger report for 29th February 1936 reveals that 50 pure-bred sheep belonging to Jack Clark of Grigsby Lodge, High Dewar Lane, were badly mauled by two dogs at Mierscourt Farm. One sheep was killed and a further eight had to be destroyed.

Moor Street House, Rainham, Kent.

Eastmoor Cottages

The timber framing of the right-hand cottage was erected when the jetties of the original 15th century house were underbuilt at the beginning of the 20th century, or earlier. The left-hand cottage was built on to the first house in the 1600s, then extended back in the Georgian period.

One of the most prosperous farming families in the nineteenth century was that of the Wakeleys, Thomas Wakeley of East Moor Street and William Lake Wakeley of West Moor Street Farm being listed among Rainham's half dozen 'gentry' by Pigot in 1839. In 1881 'Moor Street Farmhouse' was occupied by Richard Wakeley, who employed 60 men and 13 boys on his 638 acres. Hops were the main crop. Close by, at the 'More Street' (Westmoor) Farm with 160 acres, James Mansfield Wakeley had only five men and two boys to assist him.

Westmoor Cottage

The porch of Westmoor Cottage (left) is Victorian, but the house is possibly much older. This postcard view dates from the 1920s.

For many years before the Men of Kent was opened Moor Street's farmhouses and cottages had been served by the George and Dragon. Perhaps it did not prosper, for it had at least four different hosts between 1839 and 1861. It may well have occupied only a single room in one of the cottages. There were then more than twenty dwellings in the area, housing the families of those who worked on the farms or in the brickfields at Otterham Quay.

Back of Westmoor Farm

During the early years of the 20th century the Wakeley families occupied several of the larger Rainham houses. Joseph and Richard Mansfield Wakeley lived at Moor Street House, and Seymour Tanner Wakeley occupied The Limes near the Men of Kent Public House in Broad Walk. In 1908 William Wakeley lived at Macklands in Lower Station Road and Sidney Wakeley lived in Meresborough House, now used by Bryony School. Mrs Sidney Wakeley was responsible for planting thousands of daffodil bulbs, a flower she loved, in the orchards, hop gardens and fields around Meresborough, some of which still flourish today. By 1926 the Sidney Wakeley family had moved to Church House in the centre of Rainham next to the White Horse Public House.

Station Road

This view, looking south towards The Cricketers before it was rebuilt, illustrates the size of the elm tree which grew at the edge of the old school playground. On the left is the building which housed some of the Co-op's departments. The 'Rainham and District Co-operative Society, Ltd' advertised these in 1908 as 'Grocery, Hardware, Crockery, Tinware, Drapery, Boots, Clothing, Furniture, Bakery, Pastry and Corn, Coal, Meat - Home-killed and Foreign.' At that date the entrance fee was 1/- and there were 505 members eligible to share the profit of nearly £1,500 on annual sales approaching £16,000. Twenty years later membership had grown to over a thousand, and daily deliveries by motor could be arranged. Since being vacated by the Co-op in the early 1980s the three shops have had various occupants. Recently in 2006 after Flaherty Brothers left the upstairs offices the whole building has been refurbished with an extra storey added and now houses Lloyds Pharmacy and Totesport Betting in the retail shops with residential flats above.

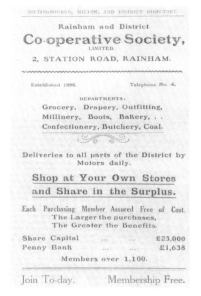

Jacob's Dairy

Next to the Co-op, at what is now No.6, were Jacob's Dairy and Ernest Sutton's Grocery, which here appears to be particularly well-stocked with joints of bacon as well as a variety of other foods. In the picture Mr Percy Jacob is the central figure, with Miss Lake on his right.

Station Road looking north

The identification of properties in Station Road in the Edwardian period was probably not a problem for the local postmen, who would have known most of their inhabitants by name. But it might have confused visitors, since only a few houses, those on the eastern side at the top of the road, were consecutively numbered. Otherwise homes either had their own name, such as Cherry Villa or Elm Cottage, or had addresses like 4 Alexandra Cottages or 7 Victa Terrace (not to be confused with Invicta Terrace). This is still true of Cement Cottages and Bennett's Cottages at the bottom of Station Road.

The house on the right of the right hand-view (now a Doctor's surgery) was formerly known as Grigsby Lodge. In the 1930s its occupant was William Clark, known as 'Snapper' because he snapped up empty properties. The dormer windows have now been replaced by a complete upper storey. Next to it, but set back from the road, was the Salvation Army Hall, whose site today is occupied by a pair of modern semi-detached houses.

Station Road

A little further down Station Road, on the corner of Solomon Road, was a baker's and confectioner's. Owned by William Stevens in 1908, by the time this photograph was taken in the 1920s its proprietor was Thomas Cramp. Fry's and Cadbury's Chocolate are both prominently advertised across the windows.

Most of the houses and cottages in Station Road date from Victoria's reign, and many still display the date of construction on the tablet bearing their name. Below the railway there were fewer shops amongst them, perhaps the most important being that of Mr Rains, grocer and draper, seen here at the centre (the white building with three upper windows). Later this became a Post Office.

Mr Rains was Chairman of the newly-founded Chamber of Commerce in 1926, by which time it had attained a membership of about thirty. The corner shop opposite was originally a wet fishmonger's but Bert Dunk, who owned it in the twenties, described himself as a Fried Fish Merchant. His shop is on the right at the end of the allotments, land which is now the Station Car Park. The small houses with neat white fences were called Volunteer Cottages - they have disappeared.

The tall chimney seen above the Post Office belonged to the works of Ebenezer Kemp, whose business recovered after suffering a devastating fire in 1917. There are still men in Rainham who learned their trade as apprentices in the joinery or building departments. The main yard was sold in the 1960s, to be replaced by the shops on the corner of Childscroft Road, but Ebenezer Kemp's house still stands next to them. The smithy which also belonged to him lay further down Station Road, beyond Macklands, but it had disappeared by 1926.

The other significant trader on the western side of Station Road was Edward Pettit, who lived at Ingleside and whose premises are now the site of Arcola Products. When he started his business in the 1880s sailing barges were a major means of transporting goods, so a 'Sail Maker, Ship Chandler and Rigger' who also supplied ropes of all kinds, pulley blocks, shackles and ironwork for shipping would have found plenty of work. Rick covers, tents and shop blinds, glass, oils, paint and tar were other goods he could provide. Later yacht sails became a speciality.

ESTABLISHED 1883.

EDWARD J. PETTIT

Sail Maker, Ship Chandler & Rigger,

Hemp, Manilla and Steel Rope Merchant.

Van and Stack Cloths, Shop Blinds, and Canvas Covers of every description made at shortest notice.

Rick Cloths made and fitted with Poles, Guy Ropes and Tackle Blocks.

Yacht Sails a Speciality.

Flags, Bunting, Bass and Hemp Ropes, Spun Yarn, Canvas, &c.

Wood and Iron Pulley Blocks and Yacht Fittings.

Mops, Brooms, Brushes, Hand and Deck Scrubs, Buckets, White Lead, Driers, Oils, Varnish and Tar kept in stock.

STATION ROAD, RAINHAM, Kent.

In this panoramic view of Station Road taken from the church tower, the buildings in the foreground on the left were part of the Co-op. To the right the house and sheds, some still in use, are hidden today by the new Healthy Living Centre created in 2006. Behind them are the glasshouses which belonged to Hutchinson's Nursery, whose business later transferred to Meresborough. The cowls of Wakeley's oasthouses by the station can just be distinguished below the distant chimneys of the British Standard Cement Works at Motney Hill. The taller, closer one was that of Kemps.

Public houses were situated strategically in Station Road, with the White Horse and The Railway Hotel serving travellers and those who lived south of the railway, while the Angel, at the Lower Road end, and the Mackland Arms catered for those nearer the river.

Like other public houses the Mackland Arms used to run a benefit club, which combined a savings scheme with a primitive form of insurance. This pub's had the grand name of The Mackland Arms Sick and Funeral Benefit Society. It had about ninety members and met monthly, on a Saturday night.

Railway

The Chatham-Faversham branch of the East Kent Railway began its service in January 1858, with horse-bus connections to Canterbury and Bromley. The station, originally called 'Rainham and Newington', resembled other country stations in having staggered platforms so that passengers crossed the line behind the train they had just left. The attractive latticed footbridge between platforms provided a safer alternative. At this period the platform could accommodate only four carriages.

The wicket gate beside the signal box in the Edwardian photograph of the station buildings enabled pedestrians in what was originally 'White Horse Lane' to cross the line even when the gates were closed to vehicular traffic. It was replaced by a footbridge in Station Road following a fatal accident in the 1930s.

During the early 1930s hanging baskets and climbing roses helped Rainham to win a prize for 'best-kept station'.
Little change took place until the 1950s. The new powered signal box was one of those built when signalling was completely reorganised in conjunction with electrification of the rail service from Gillingham to the coast in 1959. At the same time the line between Rainham and Newington was widened to four tracks to provide passing places for trains.

Sunday School Treats were great occasions. These pictures date from the mid 1930s, when the Methodist and Church of England scholars joined forces for a day at Margate. The Methodist leader was Mr Lockyer, seen on the left with Mr White who was in charge of the contingent from St Margaret's. The only shelter from the elements on the down platform then was a short simple canopy. Note the gas lamps.

The small cottages behind the children crowding the platform stood beside the oast house, and were known as Platform Row.

Locomotive No.73088 was one of ten BR Standard 4-6-0 engines built in 1951, which from 1955 until 1959 were used to haul express trains serving the Kent coast. Trains from Victoria did not call at Rainham then, but stopped only at Bromley South, Chatham and Faversham before dividing for Dover or Ramsgate. The journey by express from Victoria to Ramsgate took two hours twenty minutes, and travellers on the 8.35a.m. train from London did not reach Dover until 11.11a.m.

After electrification, and although there were now additional calls at Gillingham, Rainham and Sittingbourne, travelling time to Ramsgate was cut by half an hour. The improvement in the service between London and Rainham led to a vast increase in commuter traffic, so that by 1975 more than 2000 people travelled during the rush hour each morning. The station platforms had to be extended to cope with the waiting passengers and the longer trains needed.

Construction of the current station began in April 1989, the design being 'one of the most advanced in the region' with a projected cost being £625,000. The number of passengers using the station had trebled in ten years.

The granary and oast houses in the top picture were owned by Wakeley Brothers. It was bought from them in the early 1970s and converted into the Community Centre it is today. The annual Rainham Spectacular in Cozenton Park, first held in May 1972, was to help raise funds for its purchase and conversion.

Railway Accident

Rainham's first derailment had happened as early as January 1862, only four years after the line was opened, when the 6.40a.m. Victoria-Dover train carrying four passengers came off the rails.

Rather more spectacular was this pile-up, which occurred in 1937 as a goods train passed through Rainham at about 4.00a.m. on Saturday morning, 20th March. Fortunately no-one was injured, though the driver, his fireman and Guard Percy Gardner from Strood all had a narrow escape. The C-Class engine and the guard's van both stayed on the rails, but twenty-seven wagons were derailed, their contents being strewn in Longley's meadow beside the line between Brown Street and Berengrave Lane. Apparently the driver of a passenger train travelling through Rainham in the early hours had noticed severe vibration in the area, but by the time he reached Victoria and reported his observations, the accident had happened. The East Kent Gazette quoted an official who said that subsidence of the embankment had occurred because of recent heavy rain.

Both up and down lines were blocked, and some coastal trains were diverted via Ashford. A temporary bus service took

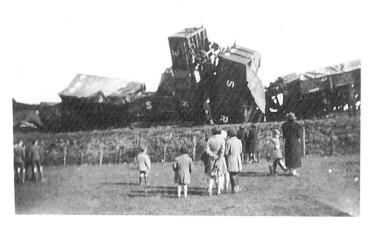

passengers between Rainham and Gillingham. Clearing operations began at dawn, and crowds of spectators watched two giant cranes, each capable of lifting up to twenty tons, clear the debris, which included wagon wheels, splintered wood, coal from Snowdown colliery and rolls of paper and sheets of wallboard from Lloyds factory at Sittingbourne. Repairs were sufficiently advanced for both lines to be open again by 8.30a.m. on Sunday, some of the spilled coal being used to make good the embankment.

Aerial View of the Station

This view shows the railway line curving away towards Newington. To the right, and parallel to it, the wide white road is Tufton Road, while on the opposite side of Station Road, Solomon Road leads to the Council (Meredale) School, standing alone amongst fields. This was opened in 1907 and closed in 2005 only a couple of years short of its centenary. On its left the Recreation Ground is bordered by young trees.

At the centre of the picture a large goods shed stands west of the station, and numerous wagons can be seen in the sidings. Here local farmers and fruit growers brought their produce for despatch by rail to markets in London or the north of England. It disappeared in the mid 1960s and in 1968 the Chatham Standard reported that work would start soon on a new station. 'After the old station has been demolished its successor will be built on the site of an old transit shed nearby which was recently pulled down. It will be equipped with platforms long enough to take 12-coach trains. It is hoped to finish the work in six months.' The resulting flat-roofed prefabricated building served Rainham until 1989.

Recreation Ground and Council School

The seven acres of land that constitute Rainham Recreation Ground were given to the people of Rainham in perpetuity by Lord Hothfield in 1897 in celebration of Queen Victoria's jubilee. It took a couple of years and much deliberation before the ground could be prepared by the Rainham Cricket Club and ready for use. However after more than a decade without their own ground the 1899 season was played on their new pitch prepared on one acre of the Recreation Ground at the Scott Avenue end. Rainham Football Club played at the other end and continued to do so until the 1980s although the cricket club had moved to Berengrove Park in 1923. The cricket square suffered far more from problems with small boys playing football despite a caretaker being appointed for ground security.

A committee of well known local gentry including Mr R. M. Wakeley, Mr S. Jelly, Mr Charlesworth, Mr S. Brice, Mr E. Filmer, Mr W. Hunt and Mr E. Morgan oversaw the use of the ground. It soon became a popular venue for football, cricket, general recreation for the public, fetes, fairs and the Rainham Flower Show. The entire seven acres were fenced at a cost of £130 2s 8d which was paid by the committee. A water pipe was installed in 1904 so that the cricket square could be watered and public toilets erected at the Scott Avenue end. A wooden structure was built on the Wakeley Road side with an area in the middle for the storage of equipment. This was still standing in the 1980s.

Solomon Road

An acute shortage of housing after the Second World War resulted in rapid expansion of the council housing stock by building prefabricated homes. These had an anticipated life-span of ten years. Most of the bungalow prefabs had been demolished and replaced by the 1990s but these homes in Solomon Road and Sunderland Square were only replaced at the dawn of the new millennium.

Ivy Street

This is another area of Rainham that has changed little in over a century. The lamp-post has been replaced, but the shop is still on the corner of Hothfield Road. It was a grocer's for many years, kept initially by James Britton and later by Edward Crowhurst. Ivy Street had a second grocery nearer the High Street, (No. 9), which by 1936 had become a butcher's. Next door the premises were listed as those of a 'licensed victualler' at the turn of the century, and as an off-licence thirty years later. Opposite was the United Methodist Church. As well as Sunday Services there were weekly Prayer Meetings and gatherings of the Band of Hope and the Christian Endeavour Society. (The new Church in Station Road also fielded a cricket team). Falling attendance led to its closure and it is currently the home of a Freemasons' Lodge.

Although the western side of the road was closely built up, only Rose Villa, the Methodist Church and three small houses occupied the eastern side in 1900. At right angles to the street was Albert Terrace, a handsome row of three-storey houses whose chimneys are still an attractive feature. In the 1920s each house was divided into two, 'back-to-back', with a separate family in each half. There were long gardens to both north and south. The terrace was sometimes disparagingly known at that period as 'The Barracks'.

William Henry Miles

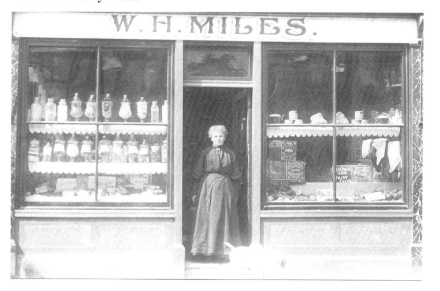

William Henry Miles was a well known Rainham personality. He operated several businesses from the Station Road area. The general store selling sweets, biscuits, vegetables, cakes, tinned foods, crisps, bundles of firewood, matches, cigarettes, ladies stockings, handkerchiefs etc was at 67, Station Road (later Hickmotts, owned by Mr Coates the Chemist). Eliza Miles, his wife, is standing in the doorway. Other enterprises included a lemonade and mineral water bottling plant in Shakespeare (Hothfield) Road and a coal merchants from the buildings beside the railway line at the station. The coal was still delivered by horse and cart for many years after this lorry was first acquired. Rainham's former cattle market was located off Shakespeare Road.

Rainham Police

The photographs are of P.C. Arthur 'Tim' Braley who joined the Force in 1931 and completed 'thirty one years of exemplary service', in Rainham from August 1938. He was well-liked and respected, and because of his height - 6'4.5" - he was nicknamed 'Tiny Tim'. He could usually be found when needed on point duty at the junction of Station Road with the A2. In 1939 he had a narrow escape while chatting to a passer-by outside Barclays Bank, when a van, its driver distracted by a wasp landing on his nose, swerved sharply across the pavement, demolishing the Belisha Beacon and trapping PC Braley beneath its wheels as it careered round into Station Road. He was severely bruised and shaken, but fortunately not critically injured.

He was a champion swimmer, a member of the Police life-saving and water polo teams, and liked to swim in the Medway off Motney Hill each day if possible. He lived in Longley Road, where he was sometimes asked by a parent towing a child guilty of some misbehaviour to 'give them a talking-to'. His duties during the war years included supervising sheep-dipping and the movement of animals from local farms, guarding a crashed German plane and taking an enemy pilot into custody.

The bicycle was an important tool for the local policeman. P.C. Braley's large model was specially reinforced, and he often carried his dog with him in a fitted basket. One of his

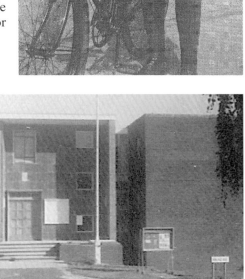

predecessors apprehended a bookie's runner from Angel Cottages in Station Road, who was seen passing betting slips by P.C. Williams as he cycled (in plain clothes) along the Lower Rainham Road. The offender was fined £5, a great deal for a moulder whose weekly wage at the brickworks was £2.10.0. It was P.C. Williams too who caught a 14-year old lad breaking a street light in Solomon Road in 1932, an offence for which the boy was bound over for a year and ordered to pay 1/6d damages and 4/- costs.

Rainham's first 'Police Station', serving its force of two constables and a sergeant, was the kitchen of the White Horse. This was succeeded by a small hall close to Church Path, shared during the war with the ARP. Premises in the High Street were then used until construction of the building at the top of Berengrave Lane was completed in the 1950s. At a later date an extension was added to the east side and the station became the main operating centre for Gillingham. The building was made redundant in 2007 by the opening of a purpose-built central headquarters for Medway in Lower Gillingham.

Pupils of Rainham Secondary Boys School tending a floral plot near Rainham Police Station in 1958.
Mr F. J. Pearce is the gardening master and Charles Langford the young lad in shirt sleeves.

Penfold Family

The Penfold family of Rainham have a long tradition as hardworking travelling showmen. This picture with James Penfold proudly displayed was taken in 1883. The family travelled all over Kent with their gallopers, traction engine and caravans. Penfolds Amusements were a familiar and popular sight on the roads of Medway. Rainham was often on the circuit and they were frequent visitors particularly when fetes were held on Rainham Recreation Ground. Many older residents will remember the smell of the engines, the contagious strains of the old fairground organ and the calling showmen, an atmosphere of an age now mostly disappeared.

Bill Penfold

A set of Penfold gallopers in use in 1943. Penfold Amusements can be seen painted along the top of the organ. The operator standing on the left of the ride is William (Bill) Penfold with James Penfold (senior) standing just right of centre on the ride. It is thought that this picture was taken in Rainham.

'Old Topsy' will be remembered by many local people, this picture showing a young William Penfold at the wheel of his favourite traction engine. The engine was a familiar sight in the summer months puffing and snorting along at a snail's pace towing the Penfold Gallopers.

The Penfold family sometimes wintered in Wakeley Road and then their children attended the Council School in Solomon Road.

David Penfold, the grandson of James Penfold, carries on the family tradition to this day despite never having lived the traveller life. His rides and amusements may be seen at many local events throughout the spring and summer months.

Lower Rainham

In the early 1900s Lower Rainham was a village in its own right having a chapel, a school and a public house. Employment opportunities were varied including work on the land, the brick fields, the barges that plied from Otterham Quay and the cement industry resulting in a considerable population. Family loyalties were strong with several generations living alongside each other. Many of the surnames of the children in the school photograph may still be found in Rainham today.

The Three Mariners is in the centre of Lower Rainham, the chapel and school were just opposite and the village general stores very close by. This small area formed the heart of the small community. These pictures show the village as it was at the beginning of the 20th century and the top two are easily recognisable today. The right hand picture is taken looking west towards the junction of Pump Lane and the Lower Rainham Road.

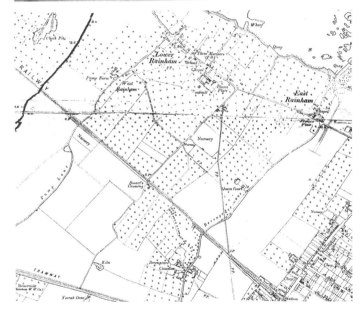

Only older residents however will be able to identify this lower photograph as the top of Cowsted Lane, the track running north towards the river almost opposite Pump Lane. The cottages on the left that came out into the road have long since been demolished as has the old house on the right.

Lower Rainham School 1921

The children pictured outside their now demolished school are:

Back row: John P. Brooker, Jack Barton, Leonard Beck, Alfie Waite, Bruce Potter, George Smith.

Third row: Morris Barton, William Lockyer, Andrew Glandville, Victor Waite, George Clark, John Anderson, William French, Dennis Potter, William Fill.

Second row: Lilly Andrews, Julie Golding.

Front row: Bessie Randall, Alice Thornton, Eileen Waite, Gertie ?, Esther Coats, Edie Liston, Joyce Golding, Alice Dayne.

The Edwards Family

The Edwards family, well known Lower Rainham farming folk, displaying their 1907 Victoria Plum harvest at Walnut Tree Farm.

Back row: Bill and Emily (sister of Charles) Booty, Bill, Eliza and Charles Edwards.

Front row: Beatrice, Charles, Annie, Ethel and Edith Edwards.

Bloors Place

Largely hidden by high hedges, Bloors Place, on the Lower Rainham Road, is one of the oldest houses in Medway. When first built, by a member of the de Bloor family some time between 1470 and 1510, the house was in three sections, the recessed part then being at the centre. The very large octagonal chimney seen in the middle of the picture is part of the original house, making Bloors Place one of the earliest hall houses to possess such a development. In the 16th century Christopher Bloor added another large wing at the rear (the southern side), but Hasted, writing in the late 1700s, says that much of the building was subsequently pulled down to make a more convenient farmhouse. The front was refurbished in 1710.

Not only the house but also the extensive brick garden walls are 'listed', as they feature gun loops, bee boles for the straw hives called skeps and the remains of a dovecote.

After the death of Olympia Bloor in about 1570 the house and lands passed via her husband John to the Tufton family, and were rented out to tenant farmers, including the Twopenny family in the 18th century and the Smarts in the 19th. An 1851 survey showed that there were 447 acres of arable, pasture and orchard, and a wharf, associated with the spacious homestead and its numerous outbuildings. From 1891 James Stewart, a Scotsman, had run the farm, and in 1920 he bought the whole estate from the Tuftons for £25,000.

After his death in 1928 the property was sold to a consortium of local landowners, James Fairweather of Newington, Thomas Goodhew of Bredgar and Ernest Mackelden of Bobbing. Mrs Stewart remained in the house as tenant until 1933 when it was sold to Ernest Gascoyne for £13,500. During the Second World War S. W. Fleming lived there and a family from New Zealand lodged in the attic. In 1950 a well known television personality Willoughby Gray purchased the property and became popular for his sketches of locals with which he entertained the customers of the Three Mariners.

The Three Sisters

The Three Sisters Public House is at the junction of the Lower Rainham Road and Otterham Quay Lane. Well situated to slake the thirst of Bargies and brick workers this scene is clearly recognisable today despite the large roundabout that has been constructed since the brickfields became housing estates in the late 1990s. Technically not part of Rainham the new houses right on the junction are actually in Swale as is Otterham Quay but traditionally this area has been considered part of the village. The demise of the brick works saw the end of the traditional employment opportunities in the area. Light industry and horse paddocks have largely taken the place of cement, bricks and agriculture.

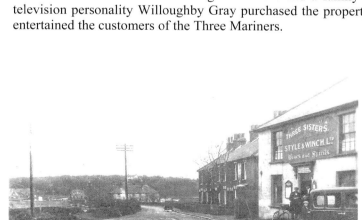

The Green Shed in Orchard Street

New flats with the name of 'Atkins Gate' have recently replaced the large green corrugated iron building which formerly stood in Orchard Street opposite the end of Thames Avenue. The main part was built in 1911 by Rainham's Freemasons, who later added a brick extension in which dinners could be served following meetings. Heating was originally provided by Tortoise, coke-burning, stoves. (It was important at the end of summer to check that a chimney had not become blocked by a bird's nest, for if so, choking smoke would fill the room when the stove was lit.) Later, radiators were installed and the wood-lined building provided a comfortable meeting place until in 1954 the Masons bought the redundant Methodist Chapel in Ivy Street and converted it for their use.

Kent County Council eventually purchased the site, which lay on the route of the proposed Rainham Bypass. During its last twenty years the 'old green shed' served variously as the home of Kent Candies, a wholesale distributor of confectionery, as a furniture storage depot for Lukehursts, as headquarters for a car sales firm, and finally, briefly, as Auction Rooms. This list does not quite exhaust the purposes served by this useful if rather less than beautiful building, for Miss Bertha Atkins, the proprietress of Marlborough House School, held some classes here just before the First World War.

Orchard Street Secondary Modern Schools

The two schools were built in Orchard Street in 1932 before the road had been made up south of the reservoir which occupied the area now the entrance to Hurst Place. Their construction relieved the pressure on the two existing schools that until then had taught all ages of schoolchildren up to 14 years old - the school leaving age at that time. The building was purpose built to provide all the new requirements of secondary education.

Class 8A of the Girls School in 1932

Back Row includes: Kathleen Ramsdale (she later taught at the school - Mrs Todd), Mollie Coveney, Nora Cox, Marion Bryan, Jean Crump, Doris Hitchcock, Gladys Pilton and Grace Dye.

Second Row includes: Jean ?, Phyllis Gransden, Kathleen Rankin, Ellen Stringer, Josephine Waterman, ? Ward and Ethel Lacey.

Third Row includes: Bessie Philpott, Ivy Holloway and Ruby Savage.

Front Row includes: Kathleen Philpott, Grace Sayers, Ruby Kerrison, Gladys Cooper, Esme Harvey, Joan Godden and Agnes ?.

Rainham Secondary Schools

Rainham County Secondary School and the masters of the Boys School pictured in 1932.
Standing from the left: ?, Mr Newell, Mr Sneath, Mr Thomas, Mr Chisholm, Mr Pharaoh, Mr Fenton.
Seated: Mr Sargeant, Mr Smith (Headmaster), Mr Nye.

Class 1A

Class 1A of the Boys School in 1932 with their Form master Jack Chisholm

Jack Chisholm (centre back) pictured with his favourite plane taken whilst he was serving in the RAF during the war.

Sports Day

Sports Day on the field at Rainham School for Girls, Orchard Street, in 1949 or 50. The huts had been built to provide extra classroom accommodation.

Back Row from the left includes: Pat Yard, Ruth ? Gloria Ward and Anne Dolling. Mr Armstrong is behind.

Front Row includes: Janet Grant, Shirley Banfield, Cynthia Croucher, Jill Palmer, Pamela Crane, Margaret Wylie and Margaret Richardson.

Entertainment

St John Ambulance Brigade volunteers 1907

Walter Rush (Draper) standing wearing the panama hat, on duty at Rainham Sports on the Recreation Ground 1907.

Fancy Dress

Children from the Camp School in fancy dress costumes, possibly for the June 2nd 1953 coronation celebrations of Queen Elizabeth II, when a huge party was held on Rainham Recreation Ground and most Rainham children dressed up for the occasion.

The Melody Makers

The Melody Makers playing at the Co-op Hall in 1933.

The Co-op Hall was a popular venue for village dances. Many people still fondly recall their first excursions into the adult world via Co-op Hall events.

Darby & Joan

This picture, taken in the Co-op Hall, dates from about 1944, when Councillor William Samuel Cox (standing under the clock) was Mayor of Gillingham. Mrs Herbert A. Edwards is sitting at the back of the nearest card table.

'New' Church Hall

Until 1937 the Church Hall was in the central part of the National school building at the top of Station Road. The entrance to the hall was down a short flight of steps giving the impression of being underground. A large supporting pillar occupied the centre and a Tortoise stove for heating took up space near the door. These together with a large stage at one end meant this was never a very commodious hall although the original school cloakroom was used as a kitchen and dressing room when concerts were held. In 1936 the Bishop of Dover dedicated the foundation stone for a new church hall next to the reservoir in Orchard Street. Kemp Brothers Builders won the contract to build the hall and it opened a year later providing a

much needed facility for the area. Two committee rooms were added later plus storage space around the back and for the next sixty years this was one of the principal meeting places in Rainham. It hosted badminton, jumble sales, wedding receptions,

amateur dramatics, dances, Sunday School, many church meetings and of course the annual autumn Church Bazaar. Finally in 2000 this hall was in turn replaced by the magnificent Millennium Centre. Modern occasions demanded better and more up to date accommodation and so St Margaret's Hall which had been built by public subscription was demolished in 2002 and the land sold for flats (built 2003) which in turn helped to finance the new venture. The land the Millennium Centre occupies had for many years been reserved as the route of the Rainham southern bypass, and it was only when this plan was finally scrapped that the narrow belt from Maidstone Road to Mierscourt Road became available for building.

Kemp Brothers

Kemp brothers were a prominent company founded in Rainham in the 1880s. Construction of the Twydall Estate began in the 1930s but was halted by the Second World War and only completed in the 1950s.

The Millennium Centre under construction in 2000 and shortly after completion.

Rainham Fire Brigade

Fire Brigade Captain Keutenius and his men are posed here in the aftermath of a fire, possibly that at Kemps Yard in 1917. Their engine then was a horse-drawn manual pump, (see the back cover picture) and the man in the cap was perhaps the driver. It is said that the horses, which normally served as sedate cab-horses kept at the White Horse, knew when they were being summoned to a fire, and galloped eagerly down Station Road to fetch the pump stored in a shed at the Recreation Ground. Also in the group is Station Officer Gibson. Medals like those he is wearing were often awarded to brigades who were successful against other local fire services in competitions, judged, for example, on their speed in extinguishing fires or for their smart turn-out.

Station Officer Gibson   **Captain Keutenius**

In 1921 the parish, with the aid of public subscription, raised money to buy a motorised vehicle, and a more convenient home for it. By 1935 Rainham's Fire Brigade had premises in Webster Road for their engine (note the starting handle). Men at this period were called out by maroon and would arrive by bike, putting on their uniform as they cycled. Local children would follow on their bikes, anxious not to miss the excitement.

'Gillingham Fire Brigade' on the side of this engine has replaced 'Rainham Parish Council' following the incorporation of Rainham into Gillingham Borough in 1929. The men were keen to uphold standards, attending weekly to practise their skills and maintain their vehicle.

After the war, when all brigades became part of the National Fire Service, the Webster Road depot was taken over by Kent Fire Brigade, and the new insignia can be seen on this engine. The siren behind it summoned the men when needed, a system backed up by bells at their homes.

There were 14 retained firemen in the early 1970s, led by Sub-Officer Arthur Cooper. His team had a high reputation, not losing a single mark in routine checks on station, engine and equipment for two years in succession, thus gaining Kent's 'Purus Verno' shield. They also won the title of 'Brainiest Brigade in Kent' when they won the County Fire Brigade Quiz in 1973. The engine, with a crew of between three and six men, was expected then to be on the road within five minutes of a

call-out, something that happened more than 150 times a year. As well as attending fires, firemen might be required to help at the scene of road accidents, floods, or even stranded cats.

Visits to fetes were less demanding, but were a popular draw which also gave the Fire Brigade a chance to demonstrate its work and perhaps recruit new members.

Fireman are seen in action here when Wakeley's barn in Seymour Road caught fire in 1970.

The barn was subsequently restored. All the farm buildings on the corner of Seymour Lane, including the original farm house with its associated barns and oast houses around the farm yard and pond, have now been converted into dwellings creating a small community right on the boundary of Rainham with Upchurch.

Maidstone Road

The oldest existing houses in Maidstone Road are the cottages and their white-boarded neighbour dating from the end of the nineteenth century which stand opposite the end of Herbert Road. Wells supplied their water.

The distinctive houses to the right of this photograph lie between Thames and Broadview Avenues. Just up the road beyond them, but not visible, are Rainham's first council houses. These form a block of four, and together with a similar block at the bottom of Station Road, were constructed just after the First World War. This was while the village of Rainham was still part of Milton Rural District. The 1919 Housing Act required Councils to provide houses at affordable rents, helping them to do so by offering building subsidies.

In earlier times there was a small chalk pit here on the western side of the road. The chalk was burned to produce lime, and Lime Kiln Cottage, which stood nearby, was until the beginning of the twentieth century almost the only house on the lane which led to Maidstone. It became the home of Alf Warner, whose wood yard had formerly produced the hoops, made from local hazel, which strengthened the barrels in which cement was transported.

Nursery Road, almost opposite Broadview Avenue, took its name from the Nursery, run in the 1920s by George Henry Page. Duncan Ferguson had a similar business, The Caledonian Nursery, occupying the area which is now Caledonian Court at the bottom of Maidstone Road.

The Broadview Garden Estate comprising Broadview Avenue, Herbert Road and Arthur Road was just one of several similar building projects in the 1930s, few of which were actually completed.

During this period the road itself was sometimes referred to as Bredhurst Lane, sometimes as Maidstone Road, and occasionally as Bredhurst Road. There had been some widening as development proceeded, but in 1933 the decision was taken to make up the road, with a 40' carriageway and an 8' pavement on each side. House owners were required to give up part of their land where necessary, and in order to maintain a flat surface high retaining walls had to be constructed where the land sloped sharply. The photograph below shows such an example.

The trees on the left, now the subject of a preservation order, are a reminder that Maidstone Road was once a lane through a heavily wooded area. By the 1930s houses and bungalows, usually set well back on deep plots, were springing up in a wide variety of styles. They were served by Mr Mather's General Store at what is now No.318. This survived until the early seventies, being known to its customers as 'Pearl's'.

Maidstone Road, Rainham   PN527

The Camp School

1955 Class Photo of the top class at the Camp School
Back row from the left: Leonard Gilbert, Bob Dunn, Georgina Williams, ?, Joy Elliot, Janice ?, Margaret ?, Daphne Ellis, Wendy Ward, Peter Stevens, Michael Dawkins.
Second row: Michael Barrett, ?, Brian Rivers, Peter Williams, Sally Castell, Michael Higgins, Fay ?, Moira Norrington, Duncan Simpson.
Third row: Peter Barton, Sheila Gamble, Pauline ?, Jeremy Aherne, Peter Oram, Neville Crane, Heather Ward, Eileen ?, Kay ?.
Front row: Kenneth McFiggins, ?, Alan Balderstone, David Brakespear, Keith Rosenberg, Terry Brown, John Turner.

Soon after the end of the Second World War it became apparent that the 'baby boom' and the large quantity of hastily erected prefab housing for bomb damage victims and returning soldiers would soon provoke a crisis for the two existing Rainham primary schools. During the war the land between Arthur Road and Parkwood had been used for an army camp housing the troops manning the air defence systems of ack ack guns and barrage balloons on the river and later as a POW camp for Italian soldiers captured in North Africa. By 1947 the army huts were redundant so the education committee acquired them as an annex to Solomon Road Council School to be run by the head teacher Mr Dow. Soon, however, Mr Rivers was appointed Headmaster and the Camp School became a separate County Primary with its own management committee (including Mr List as Chairman, Alderman Freddie Cooper, Ray Goatham and W. G. Thomas).

The huts, arranged in blocks and surrounded by woodland, had enormous playing fields and playground areas (the old army parade ground). These areas provided ample opportunity for nature walks during lesson time and imaginative games during playtimes. Everyone was familiar with the lizards, adders and stoats commonly found on the site.

The 'H' blocks became classrooms. Many of the post war generation were educated in such buildings as army huts were universally used for temporary accommodation in overcrowded schools. The other blocks with the larger hangar-like sheds became the assembly hall, dining room and kitchen with a staff room and the head's study in the Commandant's office at the entrance to the site. Many pupils have very fond memories of this impromptu school and of the staff, Mr Rivers (Headmaster), Mr Burrows (Deputy), Mr Palmer, Miss Johnson, Miss Divers, Miss Richardson, Mr Martin, Mr Smith, Miss Clifford, Mrs Hunt, Mrs Towsey and Miss Hammick. In the early days after the war equipment was scarce and the teachers managed by improvisation and scrounging from other schools, particularly one that had closed in Brompton. Singing lessons were accompanied by 'Pop' Smith's violin. Mr Smith also introduced the children to gardening, providing them with small plots where they could grow vegetables to take home. The children performed a play each Christmas. For three years this was a pantomime written by Mr Palmer, with parts for as many of the school as it was possible to fit onto the stage. Later Mr Rivers introduced the children to mini versions of the Gilbert & Sullivan operettas.

Co-operation was essential amongst the local schools at this time and for many years the senior pupils from the two Secondary Schools in Orchard Street walked up each day for their dinner in the Camp School Canteen. The meals were freshly prepared by 'Chiefy', an ex-navy PO cook, assisted by two jolly ladies who had served in the Wrens. The rough grass area was not a sports field and so weekly coach trips took place to the Beechings Way sports ground for games lessons. During wet dinner times the children were entertained by film shows using a huge old cinema projector the school had managed to obtain.

A class reading lesson. Seated in the centre is Pat Waterman with Christine Major standing next to her. Peter Terry is seated in the front right and Adrian Francis is leaning against the cupboard at the back. Adrian managed to appear in each picture taken that day as the photographer moved around the classroom.

Wigmore

This watercolour of a 'Cottage at Wigmore' was painted in 1801 by Julia Gordon, a pupil of J.M.W. Turner, while the artist was staying at Maidstone. Since there were no other houses in the area it was probably here that those beating the bounds of Rainham Parish in the early 1840s dined and 'bumped all officials except one' after making their way down Maidstone Lane through Levan Strice wood. In 1841 it was occupied by Hannah Burton but it seems to have been demolished not many years later. Wigmore Lodge House stood on or near the same site (now occupied by the Spyglass and Kettle) during the later part of the nineteenth century.

Bredhurst Road (looking south towards Fairview Avenue)

Roads could be made up by the local authority if two thirds of their length was built up, or if two thirds of the occupiers of houses there were agreed. Flints and large stones removed from their plots had to be piled at the edge of the properties so that they could be used for road-making. Corner plots tended to be less popular, being liable to two sets of road charges. Since these were estimated at £1 per foot frontage even in the early 1920s, the cost could be a considerable burden, often exceeding the plot's original price. By 1953 the price of one such site (on the corner of Fairview Avenue) had risen to £400.

Wigmore Road

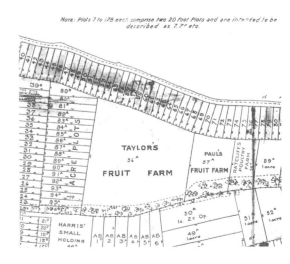

The area round Wigmore Lodge was already being brought into cultivation by the early 1900s, with some orchards and small market gardens planted, but there were no roads, only farm tracks. Even in the 1920s the mud could be knee-deep. This did not deter local town-dwellers, who for a small price could buy their own peaceful woodland plot.

A Cave at Wigmore

The bearded gentleman seen here is John Atchieson Notman, who bought an estate which he named 'Hurstcot' in woodland now occupied by the cul-de-sac called The Hazels, off Wigmore Road. It included the cave, which was said to lie beneath beeches, on an old bridlepath a mile north of Lidsing, with high ground above and a steep valley below. This photograph dates from about 1914, and although the cave still drew visitors in the 1920s it has now disappeared.

John Notman had come to Medway in 1895 from Edinburgh, where his father had been a land steward and gardener who brought up his son to the same calling. His mother, however, was related to the Scottish aristocracy, and encouraged John to books. He taught himself several languages and amassed a vast library. For some thirty years, while working as a gardener, he wrote hundreds of letters, articles and stories which were published in the local papers under his pen-name 'Hurstcot'. Their subject matter varied widely: historical, religious, horticultural, social and scientific. One of his tales had a young maiden imprisoned by smugglers in the cave of Wigmore.

A powerfully built man, he was oblivious to extremes of weather, wearing the same clothes winter and summer, and considering illness to be a weakness of character opposed to the tenets of his religion. He was a devout Bible Christian, a local preacher who was never without his Greek Testament. In 1923 he predicted 'Neither Wigmore, Hempstead or their adjacent estates will ever make populous or wealthy suburbs', but he was soon to be proved wrong.

Ambitious plans were prepared for an estate covering 336 acres, stretching from Woodside to the southern junction of Maidstone and Wigmore Roads. By 1914 much of this land was occupied by market gardens, smallholdings or fruit farms, but the advent of the war and lack of piped water supply delayed its further development. After the construction of the reservoir near Bredhurst in 1919 many 'townees' took the opportunity to buy plots (costing as little as £10 in the 1930s), on which they built huts where they could enjoy weekends in the country. A few of these huts still survive, though alterations and additions now hide their humble origins.

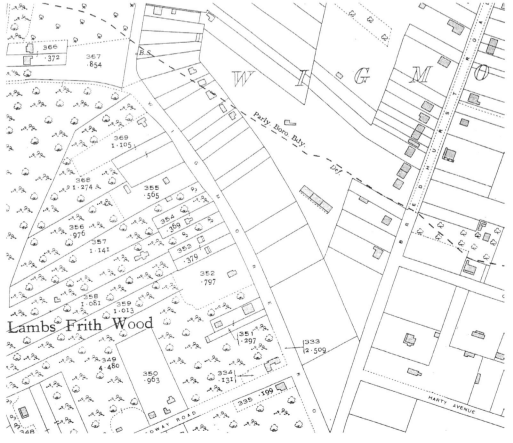

'Arcadia' Wigmore Road (marked on the plan as a crucifix shape 3 plots above the word Wood) was occupied by Lou and Bet Smith from 1959 until it was demolished in 1964 to make way for the short road linking Wigmore Road to the new A278, Hoath Way, link road.

to Wigmore

Entrance to Wigmore.

By 1924 Gillingham Town Council was worried about the erection of buildings in Wigmore and Hempstead without permission. They were also concerned that the occupants should pay rates. The Borough Surveyor visited one such hut, finding it to be a timber construction with corrugated iron roof, about 23 feet long and 10 feet wide, divided into two rooms. Since it contained a bench which might be used as a bed, some clothing, a portable stove and bread on the table, he concluded it to be a 'domestic building' for which plans should have been submitted. A letter the same year to the Chatham Observer pointed out that derelict huts, dilapidated fences and plots overgrown with rankest weeds showed a lack of local industry on which to base prosperity, but acknowledged that 'Gas pipes, a church in the making, roadmakers' plant, and buses running in opposition to each other are all indications of the desirable 'go-ahead' in Wigmore'. This photograph, dating from about 1935, was taken at the junction of Woodside with Hoath Lane, and the Maidstone and District bus timetables are prominently displayed outside the shop. A whist drive and dance are also advertised.

Woodside Road, Wigmore, from Orchard.

Nearby, at the corner of Swain Road, then called Orchard Road, William Botterill had a bungalow which offered teas to visitors. The blossom in Spring was a particular attraction.

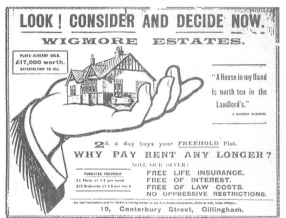

A contract drawn up between the developer Cyril Andrews and a client who purchased for £65 two plots and an acre in York Road (now Durham Road) stipulated that 'one house or bungalow only, to cost at the least £300, shall be erected on any one plot, and the plan approved in writing by the vendor'. The buyer was responsible for the erection of fences round his plots and for the making up of the road in front.

Smallholders Club

At this period a number of smallholders sold the fruit and vegetables they cultivated from a shed associated with a large house in what is now Woodside. Here they often shared a barrel of beer, for there were no licensed premises nearby. After a few years, as more houses were built, the local residents formed a club and took over the house. When this was replaced by the present building (in about 1969) there were more than a thousand members.